Celebrating the Dassel Leikarring

Thirty Years of Folk Dancing and Friendship

Karen A. Humphrey

Quill House Publishers
Minneapolis, Minnesota

Celebrating the Dassel Leikarring

Thirty Years of Folk Dancing and Friendship

by Karen A. Humphrey

Cover and interior design by Karen Walhof, Creative Advantage Design.

ISBN: 978-1933794-59-4

Quill House Publishers, PO Box 390759. Minneapolis, MN 55439
www.quill-house.com
Manufactured in the United States of America

Contents

Foreword

A bright swish of red and a swirl of black.

A delicate tinkle of silver jewelry.

A shimmer of satin ribbon tied to hand-woven aprons.

A swoop of woven braid flying through the air.

There's an enthusiastic stomp of the foot to the sprightly music of an accordion sounding a melody and a rhythm that connects this time to another time, another culture, another country.

This is the Dassel Leikarring performing Norwegian, Swedish, Danish, Finnish, and Icelandic folk dances in a setting anywhere throughout the Midwest—main streets of villages and towns, in country church yards, in school auditoriums, hotel ballrooms, church fellowship halls, and town squares. It is a vitality that brings people to the heart's tap root of a heritage preserved over 900 years.

Norwegian folk dancing, as performed by the Dassel Leikarring for more than thirty years, is based on old melodies and dances, songs and stories. And as stories go, the story of the Dassel Leikarring is one that bears telling, and certainly one that must be recorded for the history of the Dassel community and for those throughout the United States, Norway, and Sweden who are interested in Nordic heritage. For the nearly sixty people who have been members of the Dassel Leikarring, the story is one to treasure.

Folk Dances:
A Heritage to Preserve

To explain Norwegian folk dancing in Dassel, one must first learn that folk dancing nearly became extinct in Norway. The folk dance culture in Norway is very, very, very old. In fact, the rock carvings found in Østfold, on the east side of the Oslo Fjord, suggest dancing in Norway as early as five hundred to a thousand years before Christ. It is a certainty that folk dancing has been performed in Norway since the great Viking age, as sung in the venerable Icelandic ballads.

The old Norse literature suggests that ancient skaldic poems have ties to the earliest Norwegian dance ballads. The lyrical stanzas become a vehicle for the dance—dancers circling and chaining and weaving in a long line to the rhythm of their own singing. These epic Viking poems developed into polished lyrical stanzas, and then the dancing came into being on the refrain. As storytellers recounted heroic deeds, people danced to the refrain—in log houses during long, cold dark winters; in the open air of never-ending summer nights; and most certainly on *Sankt Hans Aften*—the great festival celebrating the summer solstice.

It is a beautiful picture—blazing fires glowing at the midnight twilight along the shores of any of the thousands of fjords in Norway's countryside, dancers moving in large circles, singing the epic poems and their lyrical verses of love. Singing as they dance—not accompanied by any instrument—

but only by their own voices breathing in time to the rhythm and motion. Song dances were dramatic and became a strong element of the folk custom of Norway.

The Viking Age and Norway's Golden Age ended in 1537 after the terrible Black Death that decimated Norway's leadership. Norway now was ruled from Copenhagen, and there were more and more European influences as a result. In the early sixteenth century, *turdanser* or figure dances, were brought to Norway by clerics who crossed the North Sea to Germany to visit the bishops of the church. They brought home contra dances in the form of reels, quadrilles, and lively couple dances.

The seventeenth century brought another dance form to Norway—*polsdansar* brought home by Scandinavian mercenaries returning from wars in Poland. As these new dances gained in popularity another dance form developed melding the new *pols* with the old song/circle dance. The new dance forms were the *springar, gangar, halling, pols*, and *vossrull*. Each one is a dance performed by couples except for the *halling,* which is a dance that allows men to show off their athletic prowess. The couple dances, where women could demonstrate their demureness, and men could try to impress them, developed peculiarities in each of the deep valleys and fjord regions. The variations are distinctive to the regions they represent and they are held dear to those who know them.

These folk dance forms, each of them unique, have made dancing in Norway a national past-time, and have caused those who have performed such dances over the years never to keep their toes from tapping whenever they hear the right kind of music.

Folk dancing, especially the old song dances, became an integral part of the Norwegian national revival of the late nineteenth century. The revival, begun by writers and artists, was a fervent effort to re-instate a more pure Norwegian culture. Those leading the effort believed that the tradition and the heart of true Norwegian culture, the one not lost in the 400 year union with Denmark, and the 100 year union with Sweden, was to be found in the rural districts of such places as Hallingdal, Gudbransdal, Telemark, Setesdal, Østfold, Selbu, Hardanger, and Trøndelag.

The author, Hulda Garborg (1862-1934), understood the close connection between the revival of the language and Norwegian folk song, folk dance, folk music, and regional folk dress in the renaissance of reclaiming Norway's own culture.

Garborg travelled to the Færoe Islands in 1880 to see for herself that the living tradition of song dances had never died. When she returned to Kristiania (as Oslo was then known), she formed a folk dance group—a *leikarring*—and taught the dances. The Kristiania *Leikarring* gave their first performance in 1900. Soon the folk song dance came alive to people, and Hulda Garborg was besieged with requests to give instruction throughout the country.

One of the dancers in Hulda Garborg's *leikarring* was Klara Semb (1884-1970). She became Garborg's disciple and eventually took over the cause. For more than fifty years, Klara Semb criss-crossed Norway as a dance instructor. Not only did she teach folk dancing, but she encouraged the home crafts, and the quality of that which Norwegian women made with their own hands. Especially important throughout Semb's career, was the preservation and purification of the distinctive folk dress of each area. Thus today one may see the exquisite bunads of Telemark, Østfold, Rogaland, Hallingdal, Gudbransdal, Hardanger, Setesdal, Numedal, Vestfold, Oppland, Selbu, Trøndelag, Ringerike, and all of the rest.[1]

When the first Norwegian immigrants to America landed in New York aboard the *Restauration*, on October 15, 1825, the national revival in Norway had yet to begin. Then, how did the Norwegian folk dance come to Dassel, Minnesota? For that part of the story, it is important to be mindful of Dassel's history, for that makes the story even more intriguing. There were not, in 1981, enough Norwegians in Dassel to field a baseball team. And dancing in Dassel was not allowed.

Dassel, Minnesota

Minnesota is the geographic center of the North American continent, and evidence of the first migrants goes back at least 10,000 years when the Paleo-Indians left their mark along banks of the Rainy River, the northernmost border between Canada and the United States. The earliest settlers of Minnesota may have arrived as long ago as 6000 B.C.—followed by the Old Copper Culture a thousand years later, whose people settled along the Great Lakes.

The Dakota and the Ojibwa, Minnesota's two principal Indian tribes, had well-established societies based on hunting and gathering by the time they encountered the first Europeans in 1660. Those first Europeans were two French explorers, Pierre Esprit sieur de Radisson and Médard Chouart sieur des Groseillers, who were escorted by a group of Ottawa and Huron on a trading tour of Lake Superior.

The fur trade became the area's economic baseline from 1680 to 1850. Two worlds met during this period as Europeans traded such manufactured goods as kettles, knives, hatchets, and beads to the American Indians in exchange for furs—especially beaver pelts which were highly valued for top hats—fashions of the day in London and Paris. The fur trade extended all the way from Lake Athabaska—north and west of Hudson's Bay—through the Great Lakes to Montreal. Grand Portage, located on the northeasterly most tip of Minnesota into Lake Superior, was the midpoint and rendezvous site for the fur trade. It was there, for a brief period in July, when rough and ready French-Canadian voyagers, the gentlemen Partners of the British Company, and local Ojibwa met for a time of great feasting and dancing.

"Old Stock" Americans, people from New England, moved to Minnesota territory prior to 1849. Many hoped to establish a New England of the west. And between 1880 and 1920, immigrant groups from thirty-two countries chose Minnesota as their homeland.[2] Thus it is that such towns as New London, New Sweden, New Ulm, New Prague, New Germany, Trosky, Danube, Toivola, Caledonia, Verdi, Sobieski, Bejou, and Green Isle are listed in the Minnesota atlas with Bemidji, Itasca, Wanamingo, Wabasha, Wasioja, Winnebago, Winona.

The first permanent Norwegian settlers came to Minnesota from Wisconsin, where they had established the Muskego, Koshkonong, and Skoponong communities. Norwegians migrated to southeast Minnesota—the land of rolling hills and ridges and hardwood forests—in 1852. Some, however, believe that Norwegians preceded even the fur trade as inscribed by runic carvings from 1362 on the Runestone which was discovered near Kensington.[3]

If one does not believe the Runestone writings, Jacob Fahlström a (reported) fur trader who was in the region as early as 1818, was the first recorded Swede in Minnesota. Fahlström, it is said, wandered away from his trading party and was taken in by the Ojibwa and taught Indian ways. It is speculated that Fahlström may have been Oza Windib, or "Yellow Head," the Ojibwa guide who, in 1832, brought explorer Henry Rowe Schoolcraft to the source of the Mississippi River at Lake Itasca.[4]

Swedish immigrants settled permanently on the banks of the St. Croix River about 1850 in what is now Washington and Chisago counties. Vilhelm Moberg's saga of Karl Oskar and Kristina depicts the Swedish journey and settlement of the Chisago Lakes area.

Finnish people came to the United States as early as 1639 to Delaware and to Minnesota in the mid-1860s. Their later settlements were in north central Minnesota where they were attracted by lakes, timber, and farmland, and in northeast Minnesota to the iron ore mining regions. However, a significant Finnish settlement took shape north of Dassel in what would later become the community of Kingston. The Finnish settlement stretched in an arc from north of Dassel over into Wright County, north of Cokato. In 1880, there were more Finnish settlers in this community than anywhere else in the United States.[5]

Most of the Finnish, Swedish, Danish, and Norwegian immigrants left from rural areas of their home countries, and farming in the New World would again become their livelihood. They were lured to Minnesota by letters and articles sent from earlier immigrants who described a climate and a land open and welcome to settlement. Perhaps they read the account by Fredrika Bremer, the Swedish journalist who wrote in *The Homes of the New World*:

> But this Minnesota is a glorious country, and just the country for Northern emigrants; just the country for a New Scandinavia. It is four times as large as England; its soil is of the richest description with extensive wooded tracts; great numbers of rivers and lakes abounding in fish, and a healthy, invigorating climate. The winters are cold and clear; the summers not so hot as in those states lying low on the Mississippi.
>
> What a glorious new Scandinavia might not Minnesota become! Here would the Swede find his clear, romantic lakes, the plains of Scania rich in corn, and the valleys of Norrland; here would the Norwegian find his rapid rivers, his lofty mountains, for I include the Rocky Mountains and Oregon in

the new kingdom; and both nations, their hunting-fields and their fisheries. The Danes might here pasture their flocks and herds, and lay out their farms on richer and less misty coasts. . . . But such as are too contracted at home, and who desire to emigrate, should come to Minnesota. The climate, the situation, the character of the scenery agrees with our people better than any other of the American states, and none of them appear to me to have a greater or a more beautiful future before them than Minnesota.[6]

But Scandinavian writers were not the only ones excited about Minnesota Territory. Father Francis Xavier Pierz, a missionary among the Ojibwa since 1835, wrote in a brochure published in 1853 to entice German Catholics to settle in central Minnesota:

In the past year I saw very fine oats cut at Belle Prairie on the first August and it had been sown at the end of May. We have cucumbers an ell in length, melons weighing twenty-eight pounds, cabbages of twenty-four pounds, and eighteen-pound rutabagas; winter wheat yields forty-two bushels to the acre; and one can infer that the rest of the crops are equally good. The abundance of water in Minnesota also maintains throughout the summer a pure and wholesome air, for our numerous lakes and rivers create currents in the air which purify and refresh the atmosphere and make the long summer days quite bearable.[7]

Pierz was successful. So great was the influx of German Catholics to Stearns County that even the smallest town today has a magnificent brick Catholic church that dominates the landscape for miles.

The Dassel area lies fifty miles to the south of Stearns County, about sixty miles straight west of Minneapolis/St.

Paul and forty miles east of Willmar where there are several Norwegian settlements. Dassel's pioneers were Americans moving west from Indiana, New York, Virginia, and Kentucky. They were frontiersmen, hunters, and trappers who found bounty in the deep woods. The Coleman/Sellards family, who immigrated in 1864 to the Dassel area from Kentucky, claimed that their great-great-great-grandfather, John Sellards, was a hunting partner with Daniel Boone. The Sellards descendants still treasure John's musket and powder horn.[8]

In 1871, when the first Swedes arrived at Dassel, the region was a thick, dense woodland, part of the Big Woods that stretched from southeastern Minnesota all the way through central Minnesota to the northwest where the deciduous forest met the great prairies.

The railroad brought more settlers who, in the name of progress, felled the woods and began cultivating the land. And among these newcomers were Swedes and Finns, who came in droves. The earliest recorded names are Rudberg, Sallberg, Norgren, Beli'n, Sundahl, Lindgren, Clarkquist, Osterlund, and Wicklund in Dassel. In Kingston, it was Pelto, Kurtti, Hurula, and Haapala. North of Cokato there was Kärjeno, Peltoperä, Wiinikka, Ongamo, Parbo, Selvälä, Sepponen, Kärjenaho, Myllykangas, and Ojanperä. The Swedish immigrants were mostly from Värmland. The Finnish people came from the valley of the Tornio River.

Like the old-stock Americans before them, the Swedish and Finnish immigrants were attracted by the woods, but what they found in the soil below was more than they ever imagined—a soil so dense and so perfect for farming.

Dassel, named by James J. Hill in honor of Bernard Dassel, who was his secretary for the St. Paul & Pacific Railroad, was taking on the form of a small town of the times, and Swedes were among the leaders of the community. A volunteer fire department was begun in 1880. In 1903 its members included Linquist, Norgren, Sangren, Olson, Olsen, Nelson, Rudberg, Sjoquist, and Peterson. A woolen mill, begun in 1880, manufactured *Svensk Wadmal* and was sold all over the Northwest. In 1886, a Swedish tile works was opened by Peter Johnson, who perfected the manufacturing of *kakelung*s. The tile stoves were shown at the Minneapolis Industrial Expo, 1886-1889. Johnson later traveled to Sweden to hire workers for his *Kakelung Fabrik*, and brought back Henry Hendrickson. But Johnson discovered that the cost of manufacturing was too high and the Minnesota weather too severe for the stoves. He shut down the factory in 1913. Johnson and Hendrickson remained in the community where their grandchildren live today.

When the Swedish Lutherans built their neo-Gothic brick church in 1886, the bell hoisted to the top of the steeple was engraved with the words: *Bevara din fot, når du går i Guds hus, och kom för att höra.* (Watch your foot when you walk in God's house, and come to listen.) Services in English were not held until 1921, almost forty-eight years after the church's founding, and were held once per month on a trial basis.

The Collinwood Mutual Fire Insurance Company was incorporated in 1888. The by-laws specifically stated: "You must be able to write the Swedish language, as the policies were all written in Swedish." A list of presidents during the organization's first 100 years shows Anderson (John), Anderson (Olaf), Anderson (Matt), Erickson, Olson, Lundberg, Sangren, Benson, Nelson, Dille, Nelson, and Dahlman. The list of secretaries over 100 years includes Enquist, Dahlman, Anderson (Olaf), Bredeson, Lundberg, Johnson, Lindquist, Dille, Swanson, and Holm.[9]

For all of the small businesses and light industry founded in Dassel, Kingston, and Cokato by people with Swedish and Finnish names, none is more indicative of the character of the community than the founding of the churches which became the social centers as well as the religious centers of the community.

It is important to remember in this story that at the time of the Swedish and Finnish emigration, the flame of a pietistic revival was burning brightly. Many emigrants left Sweden and Finland to escape the heavy hand of the church, and they carried the flame with them to their new homes.

The Church of Sweden in the mid-1860s, for example, forbid lay preaching and informal gatherings, even as parishioners themselves moved toward pietism. The pietistic movement, which stressed the need for repentance, conversion, and an intimate personal relationship with Christ, also clearly delineated between the kingdom of God and that which was worldly. The movement was led by Carl Olof Rosenius (1816-1868) and Oskar Ahnfelt (1813-1882). Family devotions and Bible readings in home gatherings were encouraged, as was hymn singing. Ahnfelt, who set the poems of Rosenius to music, was an itinerant gospel singer and carried the music with him throughout Sweden to various home gatherings.[10]

In Finland, the work of Laestadius was closely followed by those who would settle in the Dassel area. Lars Levi Laestadius (1800-1861) will be remembered as the fiery preacher of repentance and temperance who "set the North land ablaze." A direct descendant of Laestadius moved to the area, and when Finnish immigrants gathered in homes they read sermons of Laestadius when they did not have a preacher. Three Laestadian congregations were established in the community.

Of the seventeen churches that were founded in Dassel, Kingston, and nearby Cokato between 1866 and 1908, fourteen were Swedish, three Finnish.

The common pietistic feature of the Swedes and Finns who organized these churches in the Dassel area was the desire to draw clear lines between the kingdom of God and the world. In America, the church did not need reforming because there was not a national model. In America they could establish church principles of their own, as they perceived it. Pious Christians in this new place were to avoid being claimed by the world. This worldliness was symbolized by short skirts and bobbed hair on women, reading comic strips and cartoons, and certain activities that could seduce one into a life of non-devotion, such as drinking, playing cards, going to the theatre, and dancing. These activities, the pietists stated, were not to be part of any devout Christian home.

It is also important to remember the isolation of this community from other cultures. The closest Norwegian congregation was at Ness, fifteen miles west and a little south of Dassel. The nearest Roman Catholic churches were in Darwin, six miles to the west, and in Forest City, another eighteen miles west and north. People of Irish descent congregated there. Another Roman Catholic church in Waverly, eighteen miles east, was peopled by French Canadians and Germans. In Delano, thirty miles to the east, there stands a Polish Catholic church. And four miles south of Delano, Saint Mary's of Czestochowa was founded in the countryside with a Black Madonna as its altarpiece. Forty miles to the north, German-Austrian monks founded the largest Benedictine monastic community in the world—St. John's Abbey and University in Collegeville Township, Stearns County.

The people who settled Dassel were descendants of Swedish or Finnish immigrants, and they were Protestant. So it is that the Dassel area was nearly unto itself without outside influence. The railroad brought people to the community. But like many very small towns, unless you joined the church—whichever church you joined—you were an "outsider." And "outsiders" felt unwelcome and moved on.

Hand in hand with the pietistic movement was the great experiment to make America a more moral nation by making America safe from liquor. The grass roots movement against liquor, which culminated in the eighteenth amendment to the U.S. Constitution, began in places like Dassel, just when the village and its population were on the rise and the immigrant churches were beginning to establish themselves in the community.

Prohibition created a comfortable partner with those who sought to save themselves and their children from the worldliness of dancing. It was an easy fit. Dancing often took place in the very beer halls and saloons that Prohibition sought to close down. Street dances and celebrations were part of Dassel's early history. Oscar Lindquist records in his history of Dassel that Cafarelli's traveling dance orchestra visited Dassel for the first time on March 17, 1893. Their last engagement was at the Fireman's Dance on December 27, 1917, just when Prohibition was turning the lights out on such occasions.[11]

The law to enforce Prohibition was enacted in 1919. Congressman Andrew Volstead, of Granite Falls, representing Minnesota's Seventh Congressional District, and the son of Norwegian immigrants to Minnesota, was the reluctant leader of the Prohibition movement. But he carried the sentiment of the people in this bill from the rural grass roots to the halls of Congress. He was thrust into the limelight over Prohibition when he became the chair of the powerful House Judiciary Committee in 1919. He had immense respect from his colleagues for his background in law and his special talent for drafting legislation. Working on his own, he crafted the bill that would enforce Prohibition.[12]

The Prohibition Act was a victory for small towns and rural areas like Dassel, where the forces of the pietistic church and the Women's Christian Temperance Union were active. Dassel supported Volstead in the hotly contested election of 1920, 285 votes to 87 votes. But Volstead lost the election of 1922, even in Meeker County where Volstead lost by 1,082 votes to another Norwegian American, Ole Kvale. It was said that low farm prices were the reason for Volstead's defeat, certainly not his advocacy of Prohibition. The Prohibition Act was repealed in 1933; the great social experiment became an unhappy noble experiment.

There were changes over the years. The advent of the automobile, the coming of radio and television, rural electrification, America's entry into World War I and World War II, the Korean Conflict, and the War in Vietnam all brought changes to Dassel. By 1981, churches long had services in English, except perhaps, a special service on *Midsommar* or *Julotta*. Cartoons were printed in the very newspapers to which people subscribed and read. Children went off to colleges and universities where there was a world of diversity and thought. The train stopped bringing passengers to Dassel, but the roads from Dassel to Willmar, to St. Cloud, to Minneapolis-St. Paul had grown wider, enabling faster travel, and brought people to and from this place in just one hour and twenty minutes.

But the Women's Christian Temperance Union (WCTU) remained a force in Dassel after the repeal of Prohibition; members conducted meetings, wrote opinion pieces to the newspapers, and hosted state meetings. As late as 1978, they offered to dedicate any newborn child so that liquor might never pass her lips. The issue of so-called temperance and anti-dancing were topics for discussion among newcomers in town.

Carolyn Johnson Holje, who moved to Dassel in 1945 when her parents purchased the newspaper, said that people in Dassel had always been enthusiastic about their Scandinavian heritage. She recalls that there were people from whom one had the idea that there were definite things one should not do, and one of them was certainly dancing. Dassel and Cokato have supported community theater for years, but the WCTU still held meetings, there were no dances in the public school; children in the Finnish Apostolic Church were forbidden to watch television, movies, or films in a classroom situation; and they were forbidden to join hands in a music or physical education class to learn dancing motions. Both Dassel and Cokato were still "dry" towns. There was yet a stigma about dancing. But the stage was set for change.

New Year's Eve, 1981

The Dassel Leikarring began on New Year's Eve, December 31, 1981, when Tom and Barbara Rentoul, invited friends to their home for a special dinner. Rentoul, a recent immigrant from Scotland, worked for Control Data and moved to Dassel where they could raise their three daughters in a small town setting. Tom enjoyed lifting the sights of Dassel people with an elegance and tradition he had known during his childhood. The invitation for New Year's Eve encouraged people to wear formal attire.

While Barbara put the finishing touches on the food, Tom greeted their guests at the door wearing a silk smoking jacket and cravat. This was the first clue of the rather urbane and suave nature prescribed for the evening. The invited guests were Dan and Carolyn Holje—Dan the high school English teacher and basketball coach, Carolyn the owner, editor, and publisher of the newspaper; Charles and Karen Humphrey— the Lutheran pastor and his wife who was a member of the Board of Education and wrote for the newspaper; Kjell and Elaine Nordlie, who was a sister of Barbara Rentoul; Jerry and Ann Bollman, the mayor of Dassel and his wife; the assistant pastor Joel Swedberg and his wife Mary Lou, who was an accountant; Bruce and Sheryl Swenson (Faust). They were all members of Gethsemane Lutheran Church, the old Swedish church in town, and this New Year's Eve party was held in the shadow of the church steeple. Tom Rentoul was president of the church council; Carolyn Holje was director of the church choir. All of the guests—except for the mayor and his wife, and the newspaper publisher, who had lived in the community since she was three years old—were relatively new to Dassel.

The Rentouls served an elegant, multi-course meal on this New Year's Eve, beginning with soup. This in itself was unusual in Dassel. A guest would expect a typical meal to have simply just begun, without a first course. And it would have been hearty fare: meat, potatoes, gravy, a vegetable or two, salad (likely made with Jello), bread and butter, and dessert with coffee. Actually, coffee would have been served at the beginning of the meal, or even handed to you when you walked in the door.

This New Years Eve banquet was eaten by candlelight. Each course was savored and enjoyed according to a more European pace rather than the American practice of "hurryupIhaveplacestogo" (at least that was the general pace of things when one lived in the fast lane in Dassel). Following the soup, the main course was served—roasted turkey with chestnut dressing, beautifully browned brussels sprouts, roasted potatoes. A cheese course with crackers (not the usual soda crackers) came next. And dessert was a bundt cake set aflame with brandy-soaked sugar cubes.

There happened to be five Norwegian-Americans that sat around the table that evening: Elaine Lea Nordlie, Barbara Lea Rentoul, Daniel Holje, Charles Humphrey, and Karen Annexstad Humphrey. And there was an authentic Norwegian present—Kjell Olav Nordlie who was the superintendent of schools at the Air Force base in Rygge, in Dassel for a year's sabbatical. Kjell and Elaine chose to live in Dassel for the year to give their three daughters, Catherine, Cecilie, and six-month old Christine, an experience of Elaine's American culture. In Dassel, they would be near Barbara so their young daughters could become friends with their cousins, Heather, Pamela, and Carrie Rentoul. Early in their stay, it was discovered that

Christine was suffering from severe congenital heart defects. She was rushed to Minneapolis Children's Hospital for surgery and subsequent procedures that would prolong her life. There was much for the Nordlies to celebrate this New Year's Eve.

Kjell was born in Sarpsborg to Kaare Johan and Magna Kjenner Nordlie. His father was the railroad transportation manager in Moss, and his mother was a teacher. Kjell had been dancing since he was seven years old when his parents enrolled him in the *Svae* dance school to learn social etiquette as well as dancing. He attended dance classes for ten years in his youth and learned many forms of dancing. And Kjell had watched folk dancing all his life, especially the Moss Leikarring on *Syttende Mai* (May 17), the great Norwegian national holiday.[13] He liked the structure, the culture, and the tradition of folk dancing. Kjell learned that, unlike ballroom dancing, tradition dictated a certain way to hold your hand and take various steps. But his first experience actually doing folk dancing came when he attended the Oslo Lærerskole and was in the same class with Elaine Lea. Elaine, who had grown up in the Norwegian-American community of Peterson, Minnesota, was in Oslo as an exchange student from Winona State University. She was the second tallest woman in the folk dancing class, Kjell the second tallest man, and so they were paired as dancers. Kjell enjoyed the dancing so much that he and some of his classmates joined the Lærerskole Leikarring that performed throughout southern Norway, as well as Denmark and Germany. Kjell became a certified folk dancing instructor, and he charmed Elaine. The couple fell in love and were married in 1969 at Highland Lutheran Church, Elaine's home church, in rural Peterson. The newlyweds moved to Kjell's home in Råde, Norway, and joined their young neighbors and friends in the Råde Leikarring. Now here they were in Dassel, enjoying New Year's with new friends.

After dinner, which everyone enjoyed, and when the dishes were cleared away, someone was heard to say to Kjell and

Elaine, "Show us some folk dances." The Nordlies had come prepared—perhaps thinking of some activity to fill the time during the New Year's Eve watch. The furniture in the living room was rearranged; scatter rugs were rolled up, the antique lamps and vases were moved to more secure spots, candles were extinguished, records were placed on the phonograph, and the demonstration began. The guests witnessed two tall Norwegian people gracefully dancing their way to delicate and lovely folk music. The music had not been heard before in this community, but there was something so familiar, so comfortable that it spoke to an inner rhythm waiting to be expressed.

When Kjell and Elaine finished their dancing, they asked if anyone would like to learn a few steps. There was some hesitancy at first, but soon people stood up, ready to begin. Husbands held their wives in their arms and learned the steps first to the *strekkbuksepolka*; then the *Icelandic Schottische*; and then the song dance, *Per spelmann*, where everyone joined hands in a circle and learned the steps as Kjell and Elaine sang the dance. Soon five little girls, three Americans and two Norwegians (baby Christine was fast asleep), all cousins, long-ago tucked into bed, were peering through the upstairs banister rail watching the adults having a very good time.

The bell in the Lutheran church steeple pealed in the New Year 1982, and the dancing ended. It was, to say the least, the most remarkable evening that some had ever spent. After New Year's hugs, handshakes, and thank yous, the guests walked out into the frosty Minnesota winter night of 1982—a new year filled with fresh clean air in many ways, and memories of folk dancing—a dimension of their heritage that the Norwegian-Americans would not forget.

The next Sunday afternoon, after church, the same group gathered again, this time in the music room at the elementary school, and the dances were reviewed. The next Sunday afternoon they met again; and another Sunday followed, and they were brought together by the music and fellowship once more. The Nordlies began teaching the *gammel reinlender* and its seven turns. The group was now learning the most difficult dance—but one that included all of the basic dance movements. They had already learned the *schottische* and polka steps. And they had learned the very oldest and most Norwegian dance form, the song dance. This one was *Per spelmann*, and the Nordlies taught the Americans two verses in Norwegian:

Per spelmann han hadde ei einaste ku,
Per spelmann han hadde ei einaste ku.
Han bytta bort kua, fekk fela igjen,
Han bytta bort kua fekk fela igen.
Du gode gamle fiolin, du fiolin, du fela mi.

Per spelmann, han spela og fela ho let,
Per spelmann, han spela, og fela ho let.
så gutane dansa, og jentene gret.
så gutane dansa, og jentene gret.
"Du gode gamle fiolin, du fiolin, du fela mi!"[14]

In just a few weeks, Earl and Ronette Bergstrom Doering joined the dancing. Earl, an attorney in nearby Cokato, was born and raised in Gaylord, one of Minnesota's most German communities. Ronette grew up in Cokato, and was raised in the Swedish Baptist Church. She coordinated the immense volunteer effort that helped establish the museum of Cokato; she had an innate sense of heritage, history, and style that would help bring these dancers to a higher performance level and lead to a new career for herself.

The folk dancing sessions were family-friendly, and the children came to watch the practices and play with each other—Heather, Pamela, and Carrie Rentoul; Catherine, Cecilie, and Christine Nordlie; Karna Humphrey; Craig and Derek Holje. The mayor and his wife continued to be part of the group, though they did not dance. Their daughter, Sara, became one of the performers.

Each Sunday afternoon's dancing session was followed by a potluck supper. There were typical Dassel hotdishes along with a variety of desserts and coffee, of course. This was the beginning of a bond that would join most of the people in years of close friendship and begin a tradition of hospitality in each other's homes, a continuation and preservation of their shared Nordic heritage. This format continued almost every Sunday that first winter.

As winter moved into spring, the friends learned new dances: *Å Kjøre Vatten, å Kjøre Ved*; and *Klappdans*. At each of their rehearsals they perfected the *gammel reinlender*, which Kjell called the queen of the dances. The *reinlender* provided all of the turns the *Leikarring* would need to know for all of their folk dancing days.

Råde, Østfold, Norway

Perhaps one of the unique things about the Dassel Leikarring is the relationship it enjoys with its sister folk dancing group in Råde, Østfold, Norway, Kjell Nordlie's home town. The Råde Leikarring was organized by people who were taught by Klara Semb herself. The stories of Klara Semb and the love of dancing have been handed on to at least three generations in the Råde community.

Østfold is a *fylke,* a county that lies on the east side of the Oslo Fjord. Norway's longest river, the Glomma, flows through the county and empties into the Oslo Fjord at Fredrikstad. Petroglyphs, some of them 4,000 years old, are found along The Ancient Highway, Route 110 between Skjeberg and Fredrikstad. There are ancient burial mounds at Hunn, and at Stomner Farm. The Fredriksten Fortress stands high above Halden since the seventeenth century. Today Fredriksten, from its magnificent setting looking over the shimmering, sparkling Oslo Fjord, hosts several museums, art exhibits, outdoor concerts, and folk dancing performances.

Østfold is an area of mild winters, long summer nights; of forestry, fishing, and farming. Prior to the renaissance of the Norwegian language, the town was spelled the Danish way— Raade.

Råde is a community of farmers. Stomner stretches down to the fjord and has been a farm for a thousand years.

Many families have dairy farms, and other farms produce vegetables—cabbages, cucumbers, radishes, melons, leeks.

One of the dairy farmers is Engebreth Tofteberg, whose farm has been in his family for more generations than one can count. Engebreth's mother, Ellen, tells the story of the first meeting of people to learn folk dancing in Råde. "It was just before Christmas 1935," she begins. "There were twenty of us, including three from our family, who met with Klara Semb every night for three hours for two weeks." Ellen and her siblings had to walk two miles each way through the dark Norwegian winter night to get to the school house. "We learned the *pols,* and the *gammel reinlander*, the *schottische*, and the song dances." Two violinists accompanied the dancing, Ellen recalled. The group of twenty young people kept on for a short time after Klara travelled to the next town, but no one was willing to become the leader.[15]

Just five years after Klara Semb's visit to Råde, the Nazis invaded Norway. Their navy sailed up the Oslo Fjord led by their flagship, the *Blücher*. But on April 9, 1940, near Drøbak, halfway to Oslo, the Norwegian army stationed at Oscarsborg fired and sank the *Blücher*. The enemy invasion was halted for twenty-four hours allowing King Haakon VII, Crown Prince Olav, the parliament, and the government time to escape Oslo. Over the next several days, the Nazis swarmed Norway, and Norway would be under occupation for five very long years. King Haakon and Crown Prince Olav were able to make their way safely to Britain, where they would direct the Resistance.

Many Østfold people were active in the Resistance, including those on the Stomner Farm where the Nazis had plans to build an airstrip. They found the area too rocky, but occupied the farmhouse instead. Right under their noses, Stomner's son, Arne Grimstad, organized his neighbors for undercover sabotage to Nazi efforts. Kjell's father, Kaare Johan, working for the Norwegian State Railroad, was also involved in the Resistance but, Kjell said, never talked much about it, a reserve that was typical of that generation.

Throughout the Nazi occupation small gatherings of neighborhood young people, including Kjell's mother, Magna, and Ellen Tofteberg, continued the folk dancing they had learned from Klara Semb. Perhaps as a way to stay in touch with their heritage, to practice their own culture in defiance of the occupiers, they came together to move in the quiet rhythms of the *gammeldans* in homes, in clearings in the forest, and down by the sea. "I'm sure the soldiers knew what we were doing," Ellen Tofteberg remembered, "but they didn't do anything to us."

The modern Råde Leikarring was organized in 1959 by these people who now had young children of their own. Ellen Tofteberg's son, daughter, and grandchildren dance with the Råde Leikarring today. They became close friends, neighbors, and dancers with Kjell and Elaine in the Råde Leikarring. In 1982, two of their own—direct descendants of Klara Semb's teaching—were sharing the joy of Norwegian folk dancing and their heritage in America, in Dassel, Minnesota.

Dancing in Public

With Kjell's leadership, enthusiasm, and encouragement, and Elaine's innate musical ability and teaching sense, the Dassel friends met each week to dance—honing their skills and confidence. The rigor of dancing *pols*, *schottische*, *reinlender*; the singing and dancing to *Per spelman*, and the other song dances—as they held hands and watched each other across the circle brought them close together as friends. And soon it would be *Syttende Mai*.

The Vannland Sons of Norway Lodge in Litchfield, twelve miles west of Dassel, was attempting the first ever Syttende Mai celebration in that community. The lodge was organizing demonstrations of rosemaling, woodcarving, weaving, knitting, counted thread cross-stitch, as well as food demonstrations of traditional Norwegian fare such as *krumkake*, *lefse*, *goro*, *rømmegrøt*. Along with the demonstrations, the event planners wanted entertainment. Hester Pearson, the Lutheran pastor's wife in Grove City, a rosemaler and member of the Vannland Lodge, had heard about a folk dancing group in Dassel, and she suggested that they might entertain. Phone calls were made, discussions were held among members of the Leikarring, and the invitation was accepted.

Practices intensified. The dancers were building confidence in what they could do. They trusted each other to be in the right place at the right time in the sequence and music of the dance. But if the group was to perform on stage, they needed to wear clothes that would fit the occasion. The question was: what to wear? The Nordlies would wear their own bunads, brought from Norway, Elaine had the red and black Gudbrandsdal *rondestakk* bunad; Kjell wore the bunad of Østfold which was worn by the men of the Råde Leikarring. The rest of the group decided on red skirts for the women with white blouses, black shoes, and white eyelet aprons which they would make themselves. The men were to wear black trousers, black shoes, and white shirts. The American men said they wouldn't be caught dead in knickers. That was to change just a year later.

> Music for the performance would be a tape recording from a 33-1/3 phonograph record that Nordlies brought with them. This was the music used for Leikarring rehearsals each Sunday.

The week before Syttende Mai, the *Dassel Dispatch* carried the notice of the Vannland Celebration on page nine, and listed "the Kjell Nordlie dancers" as part of the entertainment. But the entire Nordlie family was featured on the front page that week to describe how *Syttende Mai*—the Norwegian national holiday—would be celebrated at home in Norway.

> Elaine Nordlie is up at 6 a.m. She dresses in her band uniform and drives the short distance to Rygge to join the community band. "As I drive along in these early morning hours, I see how the people have decorated their homes," Elaine explains. "The Norwegian flag is flying everywhere—big flags on flagpoles, small flags on houses. They have brought in birch branches to decorate the doorways and flagpoles. They even put branches and the flag on the front of their cars. The lawns are perfect. The flower beds are perfect. Cars have been washed the night before. The cemeteries have been visited and are decorated with flowers and flags. Everything is so green and spring-like."

The Rygge community band, in which Elaine plays clarinet, marches in their uniforms around different areas in the community. They wake people with their music, announcing the great day has arrived. "At 8 a.m., we play at the flag-raising ceremony at an old peoples' home. Then all the band members have breakfast at a hotel. Then we are ready for the big parade that begins at 11 a.m." In the meantime, Kjell wakes his daughters, gets them breakfast, and helps them put on the national costumes Elaine has made for her two oldest girls. Christine wears her nicest dress.

"Syttende Mai is really celebrated at home," Kjell says. "It is somewhat of a children's day. It's almost bigger than Christmas. All school classes, all bands, all committees, all organizations in the community march in the big parade. There are as many people marching, almost, as there are watching. Everyone carries a Norwegian flag or two. Each school class is marching with a banner that they drew and designed themselves. The young children have toy horns they blow. They sing a song or chant as they march, and everyone is dressed in their best clothes.

"Most people that are able to walk march behind the parade, through fields, to the church for festive services. Then we all parade back to the biggest school in the area. There are ice cream cones, coffee, sandwiches, cake, pop, and buns. All the school children get their refreshments free. There is folk dancing programs, games, and plays going on indoors and outdoors. . . . It is exactly the same when I was a little boy. I remember nothing different. . . . Most families are together all day long, and we always wear our good clothes all through the day."[16]

Syttende Mai means seventeenth of May and is celebrated on the day in Norway. But in Minnesota, even where there are a majority of people of Norwegian heritage, a celebration of Syttende Mai had to be held on the nearest Saturday. In 1982, it was May 15—*Femtende Mai*. The morning dawned cool and was bright with red tulips blooming in gardens. When the Leikarring met in Litchfield, Kjell reported that the weather was the same at home in Råde. (He had already made phone calls to his mother and friends.)

The Kjell Nordlie dancers performed twice that day, and had a marvelous time as well as many encouraging comments. A few visitors from Dassel came to watch for themselves, but the majority of the crowd was from Litchfield. Now that their debut was over, the word had gotten back to Dassel. On Sunday morning, the community was still intact, the pillars had not fallen, and the dancers continued practicing.

In mid-August, Kjell and his older daughters went home to Norway. He had to return to work, and the girls had to get back to their school. Elaine would stay for another few weeks with Christine who was recovering from additional heart surgery at Minneapolis Children's Hospital.

Now Dassel's own celebration, Red Rooster Day, 1982, loomed ahead, and for the first time entertainment would be part of the event at the old fairgrounds. That is when the Dassel Leikarring performed in public for the first time in their own home town.

Red Rooster Day, September 6, was almost a perfect day. There wasn't a sign of rain anywhere, but the wind was blowing just a little stronger from the north than one might like, and the winds of change were about to sweep through the streets and yards and minds of the people of Dassel. Waiting near a small stage at the old fairgrounds sixteen people were about to dance into public display. The sounds of a *gammel reinlender* filled the air from a tape deck. Some in the crowd were seated around the stage and leaned forward. Others put their hands to their chins. A few caught themselves tapping their toes in time to the music.

Out came the dancers—eight women dressed in white blouses, red skirts, white eyelet aprons, black shoes; eight men dressed in black pants, white shirts, black shoes and socks. The couples were holding hands, their steps marking time in the one-two-three hop of a *schottische*. Here they came—the pastor of the Lutheran church and his wife, who was a member of the school board; the church choir director, editor/publisher of the newspaper and her husband who taught school and coached basketball; the president of the Lutheran church council and his wife, an elementary school teacher; the assistant pastor and his wife, an accountant; an attorney and his wife, the museum director who grew up in nearby Cokato, and two young teens who just enjoyed being on stage.

One angry man picked up his lawn chair and huffed his way out of the crowd, dragging his wife behind him. Others stayed to watch as if what they were about to behold might become the downfall of the entire community.

Elaine Nordlie, a school music teacher by training, tall and erect, beautiful in her black and red Gudbransdal *rondestakk* with snow white blouse and hand-woven black and red apron, assuredly and confidently stepped to the microphone to narrate the program of Norwegian folk dances. She told the history of each dance and watched the group perform the dances she and Kjell had taught—*gammel reinlender, klappdans, strekkbuksepolka,* and *Icelandic schottische*. The dancers formed a circle, held hands and sang, "*Per spelmann han hadde ei eineste ku . . .*", and "*Å kjøre vatten å kjøre ved, å kjøre tømmer over heia!*"[17] They were light on their feet and they stomped with emphasis when the music called for it. And they smiled at each other as if they were enjoying themselves.

There was a little fear and trembling among the dancers, though they tried not to show it. In a sense they were all taking a risk in their respective positions. Carolyn Holje, the newspaper publisher, remembered that when she was a teenager, she hosted "sock hops" in the basement of her parents' home. "Friends would come into our house and be glad to go in the basement where there was a linoleum floor and lots of room. We would never dance in public in Dassel—there was no prom or dances at the school." And the story Ronette Doering remembered when Cokato High School attempted to have a homecoming dance in the early 1960s, she witnessed the president of the WCTU on the dance floor with an open Bible counseling young people about the evils of dancing.

But here they were, less than twenty years from the twenty-first century, a group of solid citizens dancing on stage, re-enforcing the Nordic heritage, and enjoying themselves immensely. When the dancing was over, two elderly women approached Carolyn. "It sure looks like fun," one said. The other woman said, "Why, if I were fifty years younger, I'd try to join you!"

The winds of change cleansed the air that September day of 1982.

And after all that, it might have been the end of the Dassel Leikarring, for shortly after Red Rooster Day Elaine and Christine returned to Norway. She and Kjell rejoined their friends in the Råde Leikarring, taking up where they left off.

Continuing

The Dassel dancers enjoyed dancing so much that they continued to practice, even in the absence of Kjell and Elaine. They had to deal with the fact that, without the Nordlies, there were too many chiefs: two pastors, two teachers, an attorney, a school board member, the publisher of the newspaper who also had directed community plays and church choirs, a museum director, and the mayor. They were people who did not hesitate to express their opinion and were accustomed to assuming leadership roles. But the group found that they were amiable with each other, and they loved dancing.

Faithfully, the friends practiced the dances they learned from the Nordlies. On occasion, they attended workshops with other American Norwegian folk dancing groups. But when others would try to correct their handhold or their style, the Dassel people became skeptical, and wondered, often aloud, "Hmm. What would Kjell and Elaine say about this?" They kept in mind that they had had instruction from real Norwegian folk dancers, inheritors of dancing from Klara Semb herself. The Dassel dancers invested in an instructional phonograph record called "The World of Dance" that taught the *pols*, an Austrian *lendler*, and the Mexican Hat Dance. Collectively, they did the best they could under the circumstances. There were no invitations to dance again.

Back at home in Norway, about Christmas 1982, Kjell and Elaine made the decision that it was necessary to move to Minnesota to be near Christine's doctors. They had heard that their friends in Dassel were attempting to dance—at least to keep in shape, so before they left Norway, they invited the Råde Leikarring to their home to put some dances on videotape. That tape, along with the Nordlies' instruction, would be the foundation and the base for the Dassel dancers and for an international friendship that would culminate with visits three times in the next fifteen years.

When Kjell and Elaine arrived back in Dassel in 1983, the Leikarring was whole and complete. The admired and loved leaders were in charge again. More dances were added to the repertoire. And then a musician came forth, one who would provide live music instead of recorded music for the dancing.

The musician was Ron Nelson, an accordion player who, with his wife Dianne, operated a music store out of their home in Spicer. Ron once had a Scandinavian old-time band that performed throughout the Midwest. He brought a special Minnesota old-time feel, accentuated with a little showmanship to the dancing. Ron skillfully accompanied and promoted the Leikarring from 1983 to 1991.

More people joined the group. David and Sharon (Thorp) Borg, a farm couple from rural Cokato began to practice with the Leikarring. Dave grew up in the Swedish Elim Mission congregation where dancing was not allowed. But he and his wife met in a folk dancing class while both were students at the University of Minnesota, and they fell in love, not only with each other, but with dancing, too.[18]

John and Louise Tjernagel moved to Dassel in 1983, when John was appointed loan officer at the Dassel State Bank. Louise was born in Ohio but grew up in San Antonio, Texas, within eyesight of the Alamo. She was of German heritage, with the maiden name of Clasen, but she attended the old Swedish Augustana Lutheran Church in San Antonio. "I'd heard of Norwegians," she once said when she met John who grew up with a great appreciation for his Norwegian heritage. He believed the Leikarring would provide a way for this heritage to continue, to be passed on to his daughters, Michelle and Amy, who joined the Leikarring for several performances.[19]

Dennis and Elaine Ashburn became Leikarring members when Dennis, who retired from farming near Murdock in Kandiyohi County, came to Dassel as a mail carrier. Elaine transferred her nursing skills to the Dassel Lakeside Home. Both are of Swedish heritage.[20]

Willie and Joyce Carlson of St. Louis Park had a summer home on one of the Dassel area lakes. Both were of Swedish heritage and gladly joined the Leikarring, happy to wear the Norwegian costumes.

The children of the Leikarring were growing older, and they enjoyed dancing, too. Kjell and Elaine's daughter Catherine, their niece Heather Rentoul, Craig and Derek Holje, Tim, Mark, and Julianne Borg, Amy Tjernagel, Karna Humphrey, and Sara Bollman performed several dances at each performance. Sara's father, Jerry Bollman, as mayor of Dassel and with his wife, Ann, travelled with the Leikarring or hosted the group for coffee after rehearsals. Their ever gracious hospitality nurtured, warmed, and made everyone feel welcome.

In the autumn of 1983, the group knew this was something that would last. Now they learned the *Giljerosen, Firetur Fra Nes, Åttetur Med Mylne, Jämstpolska,* to add to their repertoire.

Because the Leikarring knew they were in this dancing for the long term, they would need costumes—something more than red skirts, white shirts, aprons, and black long pants. There was one in their group who took up the challenge.

Costumes

Norwegian people, from every district and valley, fylke and parish, treasure the bunad of their region. Bunads— the festive costume tied to a specific area and with ancient traditions behind it—are worn, of course, on *Syttende Mai*, the great national holiday. Daughters often receive their bunad when they are confirmed, and bunads are worn for landmark family occasions—weddings, anniversaries, christenings, funerals. They are also appropriate for the opera, ballet, occasions of State, and whenever a formal dress is required. Each bunad speaks volumes about Norway—its history, celebration, and sense of place. During the opening ceremonies of the 1994 Olympic Games in Lillehammer, a cast of hundreds wore their bunads in procession and while folk dancing in the freshly fallen snow of the Olympic stadium. This vision of heritage and history was performed before an audience of 40,000 in the stadium and millions of people around the world watching from home. Queen Sonja and Princess Martha Louise wore their bunads as the most appropriate attire for this display of national tradition.

When Hulda Garborg recovered the folk dance in the late nineteenth century, she also revived the idea of folk dress. Her Leikarring in Kristiania performed in a "national costume"— a simplified version of the Hardanager costume.[21] Today, Norway's folk dancers wear bunads of the region they claim as their own.

And the Dassel Leikarring, performing authentic Norwegian dances, would have a bunad of their own, designed by one of their own members, Ronette Bergstrom Doering. Ronette earned a bachelor of science degree from the University of Minnesota in home economics education and related art. And she also was, perhaps, the dancer most invested in the community that had been her home for most of her life. Her story gives an indication of the influence of pietism on community life.

Ronette's ancestors came to Minnesota from Sweden in 1869. Her great-grandfather, Eric Frykstrom, came from Värmland, and her grandfather, Lars Bergstrom, came from Hälsingland. They homesteaded two adjoining eighty acre parcels of land between Dassel and Cokato, one mile north of the present Dassel-Cokato High School. Frykstrom and Bergstrom, who met on the journey from Sweden to Minnesota, soon arranged for Bergstrom to marry Frykstrom's oldest daughter, Maria.

The Frykstroms, Bergstroms, and some of the other Swedish immigrants were greatly influenced by the itinerant Swedish Baptist evangelists who were convinced that baptism by immersion was the true interpretation of biblical doctrine. The Frykstrom and Bergstrom families became active members of the Swedish Baptist Church of Cokato as early as 1871. It seemed that music was in their blood, and family members took part in the church orchestra and choir. Only in a church setting were they allowed to use their musical talents.

One member of the family especially gifted in music was Ronette's father, Elmer Bergstrom. While a student at Ojanpera School in rural Cokato Township he earned the lead in a school musical. But when his mother learned of the production, she forbade him to have any part in the performance. After the family moved into the village of Cokato, Elmer was lured by the sounds of music coming from the dance hall above a department store. He visited the popular place once, but his mother came stalking up the stairs, grabbed him by the ear, and led him home. She forbade that he should ever attend such entertainment which she deemed evil. By 1920, the city fathers had closed down the dance hall, citing its sinful influence on the youth of the community. Elmer found his musical outlet by playing French horn in the city band and of course in the Baptist Church where he was a member of the choir all of his adult life.

This pietistic attitude toward dancing and other entertainment continued through Ronette's childhood. She was never allowed to attend a public dance. During the 1950s, she was allowed to take part in musical productions at school, but they never included dancing. Her introduction to dance came in the basements of friend's homes, hidden from public view. There she learned the Charleston, the Lindy, the waltz, and polka. In the Cokato High School home economics department, a new teacher (from Wisconsin) taught the two-step after hours. The teacher invited Ronette with five of her friends to Minneapolis one weekend to attend a public dance at the Gustavus Adolphus Hall on Lake Street. Apparently, there were some Swedish people, she observed, who thought dancing was all right.

By the early 1980s, Ronette was well-known in the community for her exceptional sewing and design skills. Her maternal Swedish grandmother, Christine Martin, a widow who supported the family by sewing for others, helped Ronette learn to sew doll clothes by hand. Ronette sewed her first dress when she was in third grade and eventually sewed garments for her mother, her sisters, and her friends. She often took elements from various patterns to put together just the look she wanted. After her graduation from the University of Minnesota, she taught home economics in Wheaton, then at Alexander Ramsey High School in Roseville. When she married her husband, Earl, in 1961, the couple first lived in New Ulm.

Then Earl joined a law practice in Cokato, and Ronette was back in her home community where there they raised their two sons. She taught classes in clothing construction, tailoring, and lingerie for community education programs and fabric shops in Gaylord and Cokato, and she served as a judge for 4-H clothing projects.

Now this daughter of Swedish pietists and her husband were Leikarring dancers. She would be the one designing the costumes for folk dancers in her home community.

Ronette studied the history of Norwegian and Swedish folk costumes, and with an expert's eye examined the designs, patterns, construction techniques, fabrics, fabric designs, woven ribbons, lace, and jewelry of costumes first hand from several original sources. One primary source were the bunads the Nordlies brought from Norway—Elaine's from Gudbransdal, Kjell's from Østfold. Ronette studied the Swedish and Finnish immigrant clothing in the collections of the Cokato History Museum, where Ronette had been the founding director. She also travelled to the American Swedish Institute, in Minneapolis, for an in-depth look at the garments from several parishes in Sweden. On a visit to Sweden and Norway, she examined the clothing at museums in Värmland, Dalarna, Halland, Østfold, Bergen, Skåne, and the bunads that people wore to special events she attended. The research made her heart sing! She found that she was connecting to the deep heritage of her great-great-grandparents in other times and other places, kindling her lifelong skills as a designer, seamstress, and historian. She would soon connect many families to their own history and their own family stories.

The other thing Ronette found was that, if there were sewing instructions for these garments, the instructions were minimal and, of course, in the language of native sewers. Ronette had to create a pattern for the women's bodice, skirt, and blouse; and men's knickers, shirts, and vests without the step-by-step details that were standard with American patterns. Another complex issue would be the sizing for each person. Ronette carefully, carefully studied every garment, and as she made the patterns, she sketched and wrote every detail as she sewed. She knew exactly how it should be done.

An important consideration for the Dassel costume was the climate in which the dancers performed. At times, summer temperatures in Minnesota could reach 103 degrees F, with a high humidity index. Wool, the traditional choice of fabric in Scandinavia, would certainly not be appropriate. At the Cokato Ben Franklin Store, Ronette found a subtle striped cotton fabric for the skirt, and a complementary plaid fabric for the bodice. The dominant color was blue. The women would save money by continuing to wear their white eyelet aprons. Pewter buttons, clasps, and eyelets, imported from Norway for Norwegian sweaters, were purchased from a knitting store in St. Peter that also imported the Per Gynt yarn. The women would wear black stockings and black shoes. The men would wear knickers—and they would be agreeable to this. Their vests were made of a different fabric than the women's but in a compatible color. Men and women would wear shirts and blouses sewn of simple white cotton and constructed of rectangular pieces so that none of the handwoven fabric would be wasted.

Ronette and Earl modeled sample garments for the Leikarring at a rehearsal. The dancers were simply in awe of the possibility and readily agreed that this would be perfect.

Each couple sewed their own costumes under Ronette's watchful eye. She was exacting! The plaids matched just in the right place, the pleats in the striped skirt were arranged so blue became the dominant color. The skirts were hemmed at the appropriate length for each woman. The cuffs hit at just the right place for the arm's length and were completed with a delicate tatted-like lace which was also around the top of the collar. Wide strips of lace were sewn across the shoulders.

Ronette made cufflinks for the sleeves by joining together two pewter buttons with heavy button twist. The total cost for each costume, not counting labor, was less than $10.00.

And the jewelry that tied this all together was the *sølje*—the beautiful silver jewelry unique to Norway, with fine, delicate silver leaves like miniature spoons dangling from a round silver brooch. The women of the Leikarring acquired them through a Nordic import shop in Litchfield or received them as gifts from their husbands. The results were beautiful. The Dassel Leikarring now had their own costumes and Ronette's insistence on perfection made everyone, regardless of size, look terrific.

Ronette also sewed two banners that served not only as a backdrop for the group but also as an educational tool about Norway and folk dancing history. One banner had a map of Scandinavia with Norway outlined in red. Ronette attached hooks to certain points on the map so that small fabric dolls she fashioned for each province could be placed at that point when the dancers were performing a dance from that area. The other banner was of the State of Minnesota with a sweeping arrow pointing to the location of Dassel. Now Dassel had a folk dancing group that promoted the name of the community, banners that pointed the town's location, and original "costumes" for the community, much as there are unique bunads for valleys, counties, and villages in Norway.

In time, Ronette would design two other costumes for the Leikarring, each with more detail and local authenticity. In 1985, she chose a rust colored stripe for the skirt with a complimentary rust fabric for the bodice edged with black braid along the seams. Kjell Nordlie's sister purchased woven, traditional Gudbrandsdal aprons from the Husfliden in Fredrikstad, and sent them to the Leikarring. The match was excellent. The men's vests were the solid rust fabric. They wore long cotton baseball socks with their knickers, which were much more comfortable in the heat and humidity the Minnesota dancers had to endure. To complete the men's outfit, knee ties were created with colorful wool braid imported from Norway.

In 1995, members of the Leikarring sewed another new costume, this time with a more classic traditional Norwegian look, but still in comfortable cotton. The bodice was of red and black plaid, the skirt a solid black with a hem edged in red. The men's vests were made of the same fabric as the women's but had a cream colored back.

By this time some members of the Leikarring had invested in authentic Norwegian bunads that they wore for dancing on special occasions. Elaine Nordlie now had a beautiful bunad from West Telemark, purchased with a gift of money from Kjell's mother. Elaines' bunad was of dark blue wool with the long skirt, apron, and bodice intricately stitched with rose-patterned embroidery. Sharon Borg ordered a bunad kit from her ancestral home area, Løken in Østfold. The beautiful embroidery had been completed on all the fabric pieces for the hat, purse, blouse and jumper but sizing needed to be done, and then the garment had to be constructed. Sharon sewed the bunad while Elaine translated the directions and Ronette oversaw the construction. Karen Humphrey purchased a bunad from Toten where her father's people emigrated in 1854. The bunad has a green and gold plaid bodice with a black skirt and green woven apron. The jewelry for this particular bunad was not *sølje* but a brooch of copper with a spiral motif patterned after an ornament found as fill in a burial-mound on the Evang Farm in Toten in 1871. The ornament is believed to have been made between 1300 and 1100 B.C.

Ronette now owned an authentic Swedish folk *dräkt*, purchased while in Sweden. The story was thrilling to all of the Leikarring members who understood the significance of discovery and connection. Ronette tells it best herself:

In the summer of 1996, I spent a week with a dear friend who lived in Gothenburg. We decided to travel to the province of Skåne in southern Sweden where my mother's family, the Trullsons, lived before emigrating to America in 1857. It so happened that my friend's mother lived in a village on the Baltic Sea, just a few miles from Yngsjö, the village my family left. We stayed with her mother and, of course, visited the village shops. In the window of an antique store was an apron that looked familiar. I had seen photos of this apron in books I had used for my costume pattern research. We entered the store and asked if they might have the rest of the *dräkt* that went with the apron. My friend translated the clerk's response: "Oh yes, it's hanging in the back room." I was thrilled when I saw it because it was so similar to the costume I had seen in the books, and it was from the home of my mother's people. I tried it on. And it fit! Well, actually it was a little short in the bodice, but I knew I could alter it to fit perfectly. The price seemed very fair and soon the folk *dräkt* from my grandmother's home village was packed in my luggage ready to take back to Dassel. One of the things so special about this is that this grandmother was the grandmother who taught me how to sew, Christine Martin.

The Leikarring decided that wearing such beautiful costumes made them dance even better!

The Circle Widens

By 1984, the Dassel Leikarring was quickly becoming one of the most sought-after folk dancing groups in Minnesota.[22] People said the dancers were fun to watch! They exhibited an energy and enthusiasm that was fresh and appealing. The song dances, sung in various regional dialects, were unusual for performers, and they were good singers. (Several Leikarring members also sang in church choirs.) And Kjell Nordlie's own self-effacing humor, his method of educating people about Norway and the folk dances, and his standard jokes were beguiling. Audiences were charmed.

The dancers begin their performance by holding hands and entering on the *schottische*. The Nordlies led the chain of dancers—step, step, step, hop, step, step, step, hop—until everyone was on stage, then led the dancers into a circle for the first number which was often the first song dance, one of the five song dances they had learned. The music was sung in the dialect of the region.

Each dance was announced by Kjell who told something about the dance and where it was from while Elaine or Ronette put a doll at the appropriate space on the Norway banner. He also interspersed his remarks with a few Ole and Lena jokes:

> Ole and Lena were out driving one day and they spotted two men sitting in the middle of an alfalfa field with fishing poles. They looked like they were pretty dejected.

Ole said, "Lena, why would those two be sitting out there with those fishing poles? Don't they know they can't get any fish out there?"

Lena says, "I don't know Ole, why don't you go tell them?"

Ole says, "But I can't Lena. We don't have no boat."

The Ole and Lena jokes, and also Sven and Ole jokes, provided much laughter and chuckles to Midwest audiences, and also gave the performers and accordionist an opportunity to rest between dances. Another joke, used before or after a song dance, went like this:

A mother rat was in the nest with her babies when she heard a cat come creeping by. The mother rat left her nest, drew up all her strength, and said to the cat, "VOOF!" (Kjell has difficulty pronouncing w's and v's). The cat took off as fast as he could. The mother rat went back to her nest and said, "There you see, my children, the importance of knowing a foreign language."

Kjell often said during a performance, "We don't all walk alike, so we can hardly expect everyone to put their foot down in exactly the same way." Elaine added, "It's not just the mechanics of the dance that are important. You have to feel the happiness or sadness the dance is expressing."

Kjell and Elaine's emphasis on having fun doing the dances resulted in a group that was fresh, energetic, and enthusiastic. A frequent comment heard by Leikarring members is, "You look like you are enjoying yourselves so much when you dance." The standard answer is, "We are. We have a great time."

Over time, with changes in work situations and life in general, couples left, and new people joined, all for a variety of motives and reasons.

David and Mechele Pitchford came to Dassel from Kentucky. While others joined the Leikarring to re-enforce their Norwegian and Scandinavian heritage, the Pitchfords joined because it helped them become acquainted in the community. Their children, Daniel and Lorayne, danced with the Leikarring for several years.

Howard and Marlene Amundson, who had been members of other folk dancing groups in the Twin Cities where they lived and worked, joined the Leikarring as often as they could, making the trip from Minneapolis to Dassel for rehearsals. They performed with the group in other parts of the state.

Dave Guennigsman joined the dance group after seeing a community education ad in the local newspaper for the "Nordlies Norwegian Folk Dance Class." Two years later, Heidi Rasmussen joined the class and was matched with Dave—a partnership that eventually became a marriage, and they have danced together ever since.

David and Linda Thompson, new to the Dassel area in 2005, joined the class. "We found a group of people that were fun and caring, and we stayed with them. We have made some wonderful friends," Linda said.

Ewald and Leatrice Nielsen were seventy years old when they first heard of the Leikarring, and because they loved to dance they decided to give it a try. "We were so glad we did," Leatrice said. "Dancing not only challenged us but offered great exercise, fun experiences, and special new friends."

Two couples were encouraged to try the dancing by others who were already Leikarring members. Bob and Sandy Dopkins invited David and Linda Fimrite. The Fimrites loved the dancing and fellowship. The Ashburns invited their neighbors, Clint and Brenda Lindquist, who also enjoyed learning the dances and the group of friends. Clint and Brenda both had grown up in Dassel.

Bonita Garthus moved from northern Minnesota to Dassel and joined the Leikarring to experience her Norwegian heritage through folk dance.

Suzanne Asplin accompanied the dancers to Estes Park to help as, she says, "a very loosely defined sound technician," and has helped at many performances. "I have become very adept at pushing the on and off buttons, and even the volume control on occasion."

Lois Weeks already knew Scandinavian music when playing in the Skål Club with well-known Scandinavian-American musician, Paul Wilson. "We enjoyed watching dancers as I played the music, and Paul Wilson recommended the Dassel Leikarring to us," Lois said. "Jim and I joined with our four left feet, but Kjell and Elaine were so patient with us!" Lois and Jim loved the creative part of learning interesting dances, the beauty of the matching costumes, and listening for "the music to tell us."

When Bonnie Eng saw the Nordlies Leikarring class in the community education booklet, she wrote a Post-it note to her husband, Cliff, asking if he would consider the six weeks of class. He wrote a response saying he would go to the class, "as long as I don't have to wear funny clothes."

Tim and Helen Kringle had a short history with the Leikarring but it was an enjoyable time, and actually therapeutic. They started practicing in February 2009 when they not only became empty-nesters for the first time but also, because of the economic downturn, neither of them had jobs. "We found everyone to be very caring," Helen said. "The dancing was great exercise for both of us, and it became a great social outlet for us."

The Leikarring members discovered that at dance rehearsals, they could put aside the everyday cares of their world, and for ninety minutes come together to share the dances, something completely different than the challenges, chores, and chaos of life in general. People of all walks of life—insurance representatives, financial planners, school teachers, librarians, clergy, nurses and surgeons, farmers, homemakers, custodians, business women, seed corn growers, salesmen, mail carriers, editors and writers, technology specialists, attorneys, and bankers—put their professional lives aside and joined in the spirit of Norwegian folk dancing.

Each new participant learned the dances under Kjell and Elaine's exceptional leadership, underscored with patience and encouragement. And then Ronette fitted the new dancers with the Dassel costumes. They performed with the Leikarring on stage when they feel comfortable doing so.[23]

Over time, the Leikarring has been invited and performed for such well-known state and regional events as Scandinavian Days at the Iron Range Interpretative Center in Chisholm; the Festival of Nations in St. Paul; the Hjemkomst Festival in Moorhead, where Roland Dille, a Dassel native and president of Moorhead State University, watched with a great deal of interest and pride; Svenskarnas Dag in Minnehaha Park, Minneapolis; and Norway Day in Minneapolis. The Leikarring has been the featured folk dancing group at the Syttende Mai Festival in Stoughton, Wisconsin; four times at the Scandinavian June Weekend at Estes Park, Colorado; and three times at the autumn Svensk Hylllningsfest Celebration in Lindsborg, Kansas. In addition to Stoughton, the Dassel Leikarring has highlighted Syttende Mai festivals in Hudson, Wisconsin; Litchfield, Sunberg, Minneapolis, Atwater, Wanamingo, Willmar, Benson, Owatonna, Minnesota; and seven times in the little Norwegian community of Milan, Minnesota.

They have carefully danced on flatbed trucks in parades in Lindsborg, Spicer, Stoughton. They marched in the first-ever Red Rooster Day Parade in Dassel where, it was feared, that there would be so many people participating in the parade that, like in Lake Woebegon, everyone would have to take turns so that one group could watch the parade while the other made the parade. It didn't happen that way, but thought was given to the possibility nevertheless.

They danced at the opening of the Kaffistova at the Radisson South Hotel; the Minneapolis Farm Broadcasters Annual Convention in Bloomington, the State Federation of Women's Clubs, and several Norwegian *lag* and *stevne* gatherings throughout Minnesota.

In 1994, the Dassel Leikarring contributed to international understanding at the Minnesota State Fair. To celebrate the world's cultural environment, the Department of Natural Resources presented a music and dance festival on their outdoor stage. All in native costume, the program featured Hindu dancers, African drummers, American Indian dancers, songs by Jewish children, Hmong children performing traditional southeast Asia dancing, a break-dancing group from a Bahai fellowship, and the Dassel Leikarring who performed two traditional Norwegian dances.

The Leikarring was called on to perform at a major Midsummer Festival of Music at Hyland Park in Minneapolis, where an authentic Swedish wedding took place. The Leikarring marched in the bridal procession to music by Swedish fiddlers. Hardanger fiddlers provided the bridal march music during a mock Norwegian wedding in Lakeville, Minnesota on a perfect May evening, complete with bonfire. The Leikarring performed for all the guests.

The Dassel Leikarring has been exceptionally supportive of their hometown. School, church, nursing homes, and civic organizations have all been the beneficiaries of the Leikarring's glad willingness to help in any way they can. The partnership between the Leikarring and the Dassel Area Historical Society Museum has been especially significant.

Carolyn Holje, who, with her family, was among the earliest members of the Leikarring, is now the director of the Dassel museum. For almost thirty years, Carolyn and Dan Holje were the owners, editors and, publishers of the *Dassel Dispatch* and *Cokato Enterprise*. Carolyn has observed through several lenses what the folk dancing group has meant to the community. "I am so proud of the Leikarring," she said. "The group is preserving the cultural heritage of this Scandinavian community; they represent our community so well and with distinction wherever they dance—throughout Minnesota, six other states, and in Norway as well. They have been marvelous ambassadors for us all. But even more than that," Carolyn continues, "they willingly give of their time and talents to our whole community. They have made Taste of Dassel, sponsored by the Dassel Area Historical Society, a yearly event that features Scandinavian food some of which the Leikarring provides. Not only do they bring food, they provide the entertainment! The Leikarring also helps with additional fundraising for the museum by performing at the Mushroom building every summer."[24] Carolyn went on to say that it seems most appropriate that the Leikarring holds its weekly practices at the Dassel History and Ergot Museum because they are key to preserving the heritage of the community.

Music

The tunes sound so familiar—a melody that sends the sound stretching to both mind and heart. The Norwegian dance music is performed on the prairies, in community halls and fairgrounds; at historic sites of log cabins and turn-of-the-century white frame houses, at churches small and large, under waving flags in parks and town squares. The Leikarring came to know this music to the core of their memory—both mind and feet! Kjell has said about folk dancing music, "What the brain forgets, the feet remember, and the music will tell you."

The music has to fit the dance, and the dances the Leikarring perform are from Vestfossen, Eiker, Holt, Aust-Agder, Buskerud, Asker, Ringerike, Sogn, Gjemnes, Nordmøre, Namdale, Telemark, Hordaland, and Østfold in Norway. There are Finnish, Swedish, Danish, and Icelandic tunes as well. Some of the tunes are well-known by folk musicians in Minnesota; others had to be learned by the musicians. But first, the dancers had to master the steps themselves.[25]

The Nordlies were able to acquire the music for the dances either on sheet music, or on recordings by such musicians as Aage Grundstad and the Boston Scandinavian Ensemble. If recorded music was not available, Elaine recorded herself playing the melody on the piano; then she could help Kjell teach the dances.

Ron Nelson knew most of the music and had the remarkable ability to quickly learn music if it was new to him. Occasionally, Dick Rees, a host of a Twin Cities Scandinavian radio program, played for the Leikarring on his button and piano accordions, and occasionally on his fiddle.

When Nelson or Rees were not available, the Leikarring used recorded music. A new sound system was recently purchased with a grant from the Southwest Minnesota Arts and Humanities Council. The music for the recordings was chosen from Aage Grundstad's Ensemble *Norske Tur og Folkedanser* numbers 1,2, and 4; Dick Rees' *Old Time Squeeze Box Favorites*; Lindesnes Trekkspilsklubb *Vi seiler vidare* number 6; Boston Scandinavian Ensemble's *Gammeldanser*; Christiania Tur og Runddansensemble's *Norske Turdanser*.

Hands Across the Sea

The Dassel Leikarring first realized that their dancing was means of international understanding when four couples travelled to Norway in 1985 to meet Kjell and Elaine's friends in the Råde Leikarring.

The Americans were warmly welcomed, much like long-lost cousins who had finally come for a visit. They stayed in the homes of the Råde Leikarring, and they too had young families. It was a beautiful match. The Americans experienced a Norwegian breakfast—hearty bread, cheese, boiled eggs, ham, pickles, cucumbers, tomatoes, and coffee, strong enough to float a horse shoe, with real cream. It was June, the season for strawberries which were sweet and succulent. The families took walks together in the nearby woods and through their flower gardens. They toured Engebreth and Grete Weel Tofteberg's dairy farm, and Vidar and Reidun Sørlie's vegetable farm. Of special interest to the women was the visit to the Husfliden— the place of local handcrafts and authentic bunads from the region. Kjell's sister and her husband welcomed her brother's American friends to lunch at their farm on Rostadveien in Fredrikstad. Here the Dassel visitors saw the site where the Tune ship was excavated in 1867. Built in 900, the Tune ship is now on display at the famous Viking Ship Museum on Bygdøy, just outside of Oslo. The museum is one of the great cultural attractions in all of Norway. On the Rostadveien farm, the children enjoyed imagining how it must have been for a Viking ship to be buried on a hilltop above the fjord.

Råde's *Bøndernes Hus* (Råde's Farmers' Hall) was the scene of the first official meeting of the two Leikarrings. It was a comfortable setting for the rural Minnesotans, the place where the Råde group rehearsed each week. The American guests were warmly welcomed with gracious hospitality. First, coffee was served, a bountiful Norwegian *kaffe*, with beautiful and hearty open-faced sandwiches, and those fresh strawberries brought to the event from local farms and gardens. This was the evening that the "world's best dessert" was introduced to the Americans—a scrumptious dessert of meringue, centered with rum pudding, almonds, and whipped cream. Candles were lit on each table, and someone had placed freshly picked flowers in simple glass vases on each table, too.

After everyone became acquainted by telling a little bit about themselves, it was time to begin the dancing. As soon as accordionist Per Auberg started to play, Ron Nelson joined in, and the American dancers danced each dance with their new international friends. This was proof of Kjell's statement, "Our group has learned the same style of dancing that the people living in Norway know. It is neat that we can all dance together and learn from each other."

There was one dance, however, that the Dassel folks had difficulty with and that was the *Østfold Springar*. The Råde group took a good deal of pride in this dance and were part of an effort to save the dance from becoming lost to folk dancers of the future. They were even part of a day-long *springar* competition when folk dancers from across Østfold went on tour to perform the dance in towns throughout the province on a variety of surfaces—asphalt parking lots, cobblestones in the centrum, grass in front of museum buildings, a wooden stage. The Dassel visitors went along on this tour, keeping to the edge of the dancing circle at each venue, away from the judges' eyes. Everyone was very proud when Engebreth and Grete were in the top ten of the dancers. Eventually the Dassel dancers learned the dance well enough to include it in their repertoire back home, even performing it as the opening for a program. The *Østfold Springar* has not been lost!

The Dassel Leikarring had the opportunity to return the hospitality when the Råde Leikarring visited Dassel in May 1988. To help pay for their trip, members of the Råde group scrubbed the local nursing home from top to bottom that spring. Several of the couples had never been to the U.S., and they were coming to Dassel to put their foot on American soil for the first time. The official performance was on stage at the Dassel Elementary School to a packed auditorium. It was one of the hottest nights of the year, and the auditorium was without air conditioning. The Norwegian dancers, wearing their wool bunads, exclaimed they had never experienced such weather! And it wasn't so comfortable for the Dassel dancers either, even though their costumes were of a lighter fabric. But the performance went forward. Each Leikarring performed separately, then joined together in several dances. Everyone toughed it out, and no one fainted. At the conclusion of the program the audience gave the dancers a standing ovation. In a brief ceremony, long-stemmed American Beauty roses were presented to each Norwegian couple who came forward as their names were called. Ice cold lemonade, coffee, and Scandinavian cookies made by friends of the Leikarring— Dorothy Danielson, Violet Dahlman, and Ann Bollman—were served to everyone following the performance.

The Dassel Leikarring members planned a series of events for their sister folkdancing group's first visit to America. At the Nordlie home on the south shore of Spring Lake, the guests from Råde were guests at a potluck picnic. The Dassel Leikarring hired a driver and a bus to Taylors Falls where a paddleboat waited to take the Norwegians and Americans on an evening excursion on the St. Croix River with dancing and a live band. Later in the week, the Leikarrings drove to the open air heritage museum at Montevideo for a memorable evening performance before the local Sons of Norway. In between there were tours of Dassel area farms, a trip to the Ridgedale shopping mall, and a trip to the Mille Lacs Indian Museum. Then a farewell supper and party hosted by the Doerings at their home on the north shore of Lake Washington brought the whirlwind week to a close.

The Dassel Leikarring has hosted three Swedish folk dancing groups. On June 28, 1984, the Vessigebro Dragspelklubb from Vessigebro in Halland (twenty-five couples) visited. When the Spelman och Dansare fra Dal, in Dalsland, came on July 24, 1986, a folk dancing workshop was held. In July 1996, the Leikarring hosted Osterøy Spel og Dansarlag from the island municipality of Osterøy on the west coast of Norway, not far from Bergen. And a folk dancing group from Romerike came through Dassel on their way to perform at Høstfest in 2007. The groups practiced together at the Dassel Museum. On June 4, 2001, the Swedish high school folk dancers from Lindsborg, Kansas, stayed and performed in the community.

In every case, Dassel and Cokato area residents opened their homes to host the guests overnight, and brought them to the appropriate places for dance rehearsals or tours. Inevitably the guests and their hosts enjoyed a potluck, or a cookout at someone's home where typical Midwestern food and hospitality were on magnificent display.

And over the years, such members of the Råde Leikarring as Jan Petter Olsen and Anne Enger, Vidar and Reidun Sørlie, Engebreth and Grete Tofteberg, Per and Kari Hvidsten, Inger Skaar and Ivar Hansen have made independent visits to Dassel and joined their American counterparts in performance. In 1996, when Earl and Ronette were visiting the Toftebergs on their farm in Råde, the Doerings stepped in an emergency to help the Råde Leikarring with performances in three local villages. Råde members loaned the Doerings bunads for the occasion, which just happened to fit Ronette and Earl perfectly. And because they had learned the dances from Kjell and Elaine, no one in the audience knew that there were two Americans filling in.

Holding the Heritage Close

Kjell Nordlie says, "It is wonderful when people care about preserving their heritage. I think you lose some of yourself if you don't."

Norwegian folk dancing has its roots in a rural culture, with people who gathered in farmer halls. Indeed, it was the rural culture that Hulda Garborg advocated in the late nineteenth century and beginning of the twentieth century. It was honest pride in the rural culture, built on real people who in their farm homes baked bread, wove cloth, milked cows, grew vegetables, and put up hay. The folk costumes developed from already established designs and from the fabrics of solid clothes of rural Norway: homespun, cross stitch, and embroidery stitched by firelight during the dark winters or by window light during long summer evenings. It was from the rural culture that people emigrated to the Midwest—to Wisconsin, Iowa, Minnesota, North Dakota, and South Dakota. Most of the members of the Dassel Leikarring are descended from these people.

Leikarring members have said they were attracted to the dancing by their own family stories discovered while researching family history. Dancing has inspired others to begin their family histories. The list of Leikarring members and the stories of their ancestors coming to America is a great story of the American immigration itself. They came from places in Norway such as Lunde, Kviteseid, Flaabygd, Hasselied, Tuddal, Stavanger, Gudvangen, Tingvoll, Oslo, Vestre Slidre, Bergen, Kvinnherad, Bua, Bagn, Toten, Snertingdal, and Holje; from Edleskog, Västra

Torsas, Bredsattra, Skephult, Tranemo, Gräsmark, and Yngsjö in Sweden, as well as England, Germany, and Wales. Great-grandparents and grandparents of the Leikarring members said good-bye to all whom they loved, and gave up much to start new lives. And somehow, their progeny met each other in Dassel where they began learning folk dance.[26]

One could say that preserving, enhancing, bringing to light the heritage of a people is important to understanding who we are as individuals. For some members of the Dassel Leikarring, this is an important aspect of the folk dancing. And Dassel was one of the communities in the 1980s where traces of Swedish could still be heard and people still talked about their heritage—recalling the old songs and hymns, family ancestral ties, art and craft of Sweden, and heritage baking. Baking became a fury during Advent with such Scandinavian delicacies as *spritz, fattigman, lefse,* flatbread, *krumkake, goro, sandbakkels, limpa,* Finnish tarts, fruit soup, *riskrem,* and potato sausage. Lutefisk was sold in local grocery stores. In the early 1980s, the Cokato Dassel Rotary organized a lutefisk dinner to raise money for scholarships. The Leikarring performed at the first dinner and for several dinners after, to set the atmosphere for the eating. The music was perfect for a cold December night, usually the first Saturday of December. The music of the dancing touched their hearts and minds. For several Leikarring members, the heritage soul food filled their senses.

Ronette Doering founded an entire career and a new business after she designed the first costume for the Leikarring. When the Leikarring performed for the annual *Syttende Mai* celebration at Augustana Homes in Litchfield, she was approached by Marge Hellzen, owner of *Ports of Scandinavia,* an importer and distributor of Scandinavian needlework and gifts. Hellzen knew there was a formidable market in the United States for Scandinavian patterns with American sizing and instructions, and she had been looking for someone to design a series of patterns they could market. After the performance, Hellzen approached Ronette and asked if she would be willing to publish the pattern she had designed. Ronette agreed, and her patterns were published in March 1987. For almost twenty years, under Olde Country Costumes by Doering Designs, Ronette not only published patterns for men, women, children, and dolls, but created jewelry from Norwegian pewter buttons, and imported wool braid, cotton ribbons, and some fabrics directly from factories in Norway and Sweden. She began advertising in sewing magazines; through the ads she received requests from enthusiasts in all fifty states, 200 stores, and a store in Australia as well.[27]

The interest in the dances of Norway, and the teaching of Kjell and Elaine has extended well beyond Minnesota. The Dassel Leikarring has been videoed as a teaching tool for Sons of Norway, and the videos are used extensively throughout the United States as part of a wider education program. Kjell and Elaine have taught folk dancing in Brookings, South Dakota; and twice in Dallas when the Norwegian Society of Texas hosted groups from all corners of the state for instruction.

Yet beyond the family heritage, food heritage, folk dress, and the joy of dancing, there is the fact that the Dassel Leikarring is also caring for the heritage of the Norwegian song dances. One of the very favorites of the Leikarring is the famous love story of *Bendik and Årolilja*, a saga from the Middle Ages in Norway (1066-1300) preceding Shakespeare's similar saga of Romeo and Juliet (1597) by at least 300 years.

According to legend, the story takes place at the Urnes stave church—the Queen of the Stave churches—high, high above the Luster fjord in Sogn, and built in the 1100s. In early times, it is said, people could even point to the place where the gallows had been and the place where Årolilja took her own life.[28] Bendik is buried on one side of the church, Årolilja on the other, and it is said that a lily on each grave grows above the church walls and entwines at the top. The dance is filled with a certain mood and somberness as the dancers sing the tragic love story, unaccompanied by instruments. The Leikarring sings the story in Norwegian:

Bendik rid åt sølando
Ville han skoda møy,
Han var ikkje lagje te atte koma,
Difor so laut han døy
Årolilja, kvi søve du så lengje?

Om dagjen rid Bendik i skogjen ut,
og veider den ville hjort,
om notti vitjar han jomfruva
med åst og elskogs-ord
Årolilja, kvi søve du så lengje?

The dancers form a circle, holding hands, and use Faroe steps. They sing the verse. Each woman takes a small step towards the center on her right foot, then places it by the side of her left foot. The men step in farther than the women and join hands. Each man bends his knee a little and straightens it as he steps back on the left foot, at the same time lifting his arms forward and upward, and then softly down. At the same time, each woman bending her knee, and bowing her head, takes a step inward as the women pass under the men's arms, then join hands and raise their heads. At the same time each woman places her right foot to the side of her left foot. The women now repeat the steps and movements of the men, and the men those of the women. They stand still for a moment, then begin the verse again. At the last verse, the men stand still and lift the arms, palm to palm, forward and upward while they sing the word "Årolilja," keeping their arms raised as they sing the last words. At the same time the women, standing close behind and between the men, lift their arms, crossing them on their breasts and slowly lowering the head until their chins are lowered. The dancers remain thus until the last note fades away. The men then, in silence lower their arms, and raise their heads. At the same time, the women slowly lower their arms and raise their

heads. The movement represents a lily opening and closing.[29]
The entire ballad is several verses long:

> Bendik rode to Sølando,
> There a maid to find,
> But never will he ride back again:
> Cruel fate dooms him there to die:
> Årolilja, why sleep you so long?
>
> Young Bendik dwelt in the King's castle
> More than a week or two;
> He fell in love with the King's daughter,
> Maiden so fair and true.
> Årolilja, why sleep you so long?
>
> The King he built a drawbridge high
> Built it of shining gold.
> "Whoever crosses this bridge shall die,
> Be he prince or warrior bold."
> Årolilja, why sleep you so long?
>
> Answered the King young Bendik bold,
> Thus boldly answered he,
> "It is I who will cross your bridge of gold
> E'en if I die presently."
> Årolilja, why sleep you so long?
>
> Then Bendik tells her of his love,
> Praises her beauty so rare:
> "Like ripe yellow apples bending low
> Are the braids of your golden hair."
> Årolilja, why sleep you so long?
>
> Down came the fist of the Danish King:
> "Now shall young Bendik die.
> Not all the wealth of the wide, wide world
> Pardon for him can buy."
> Årolilja, why sleep you so long?

Cries out the maiden to the King,
"Spare, Father, spare my love."
"Cease, daughter, cease, ere this sword of mine
Be dripping with maiden's blood."
Årolilja, why sleep you so long?

Shadows fell on the whole wide world,
All living things in their pain,
The leaves and the deer and the silent birds
Begging his life in vain.
Årolilja, why sleep you so long?

There beside the lonely church
Beautiful Bendik was slain:
High, high in the tower she pined and died,
Fair broken-hearted maid.
Årolilja, why sleep you so long?

On the north side young Bendik sleeps
On the south Årolilja lies,
And out of their graves two lilies grow,
Marvel to sorrowing eyes.
Årolilja, why sleep you so long?

High o'er the church the lilies grow,
Each to each other they cling;
A-twining together the flowers they blow,
Foretelling the doom of the King.
Årolilja, why sleep you so long?[30]

Choice Scandinavian Recipes from the Dassel Leikarring

Friendship is one of the great gifts of the Dassel Leikarring—friendships built on the joy of dancing and shared over coffee and a meal in each other's homes. Here are favorite recipes.

The Leikarring Kaffe Table

Riskrem

Cook 1-1/3 cups water with 1/2 tsp. salt and 1 tbsp. margarine or butter.

Put in 3/4 cup rice. Cover and cook on low heat for ten minutes until water is absorbed.

Add 3 cups milk. Cover and cook on low heat for about 30 minutes or until thickened.

Stir in 3-4 tbsps. sugar.

Allow to cool overnight in the refrigerator.

On the following day, sweeten 1 pint of heavy cream with 3-4 tbsps. sugar and 1 tbsp. vanilla sugar (or vanilla). Whip all together and combine with the cold rice pudding.

Return to the refrigerator until ready to serve.

Serve with a spoonful of raspberry or strawberry sauce.

Elaine Nordlie

Swedish Ginger Cookies

1 cup butter

1-1/2 cup sugar

1 egg

1-1/2 tbsps. grated orange peel

2 tbsps. dark corn syrup

1 tbsp. water

3-1/4 cups flour

2 tsps. soda

2 tsps. cinnamon

1 tsp. ginger

1/2 tsp. cloves

Blanched almonds

Thoroughly cream butter and sugar. Add egg and beat until light and fluffy.

Add orange peel, corn syrup, and water. Mix well.

Sift together dry ingredients; stir into creamed mixture.

Chill dough thoroughly.

On lightly floured surface, roll to 1/8 inch thick. Cut in desired shapes with a floured cookie cutter. (I use little pig shapes.) Place 1 inch apart on ungreased baking sheet. Top each cookie with half of a blanched almond.

Bake in 375 degree oven or 8 to 10 minutes. Cool on rack.

Makes about 8 dozen cookies.

Note: For a sparkly look, sprinkle rolled dough with sugar before baking.

Leatrice Nielsen

Golden Spice Cake

1/2 cup butter (scant)

2 eggs

3/4 cup syrup

1/4 cup orange marmalade

3/4 tsp. ginger

2 tsps. baking powder

1-1/2 cups flour

2/3 cup light cream

Cream butter until soft. Add eggs, syrup, and orange marmalade.

Blend well.

Add ginger and baking powder to the flour.

Add dry mixture to the butter mixture alternately with cream.

Mix thoroughly.

Pour into a greased 1-1/2 quart loaf pan.

Bake at 350 degrees for about 30 minutes.

Linda Thompson

Honey Loaf Cake

4 eggs, separated

1-1/8 cup sugar

7 tbsps. butter

7/8 cup honey

1/4 tsp. cloves

1/4 tsp. pepper

1/2 tsp. ginger

1 tsp. baking powder

1-2/3 cups flour

Beat egg yolks and sugar until well mixed.

Melt the butter and mix with the honey, then add to egg mixture.

Combine dry ingredients and add, blending fully.

Whip egg whites until stiff peaks form, and fold into batter.

Pour the batter into a greased 1-1/2 quart paper lined loaf pan. Bake at 300 degrees about 50 minutes. Decorate with chocolate glacé and almonds, if desired.

Linda Thompson

Christmas Bread

1-1/8 cups butter

2 cups sugar

3 eggs

4 cups flour

1 tsp. cardamom

4 tsps. vanilla sugar

4 tsps. baking powder

2 cups coffee cream

7/8 cup citron, finely chopped

1-1/8 cups raisins

Cream butter and sugar until light and fluffy. Add the eggs, one at a time. Mix flour (save out a little to mix with fruit to prevent it from sinking to the bottom of pan), cardamom, baking powder, and vanilla sugar; add to butter mixture alternately with cream.

Add fruit. Stir well. Preheat oven to 350 degrees. Grease two loaf pans and line the bottoms with wax paper. Pour batter into pans and bake about one hour. Cool on rack. Makes two loaves.

Linda Thompson

Orange Loaf Cake

2 eggs

2/3 cup sugar

1/2 cup butter (scant)

1 cup orange marmalade

1/2 cup milk (scant)

3/4 cup raisins

2 cups flour (scant)

2 tsps. baking powder

Beat eggs and sugar until light and fluffy. Melt butter, cool slightly, and whip together with the egg mixture. Add marmalade, milk, and raisins. Mix well. Stir in flour and baking powder and mix thoroughly. Grease a large bread pan and pour the batter into the pan. Bake in 350 degree oven on the lowest rack for 30 to 60 minutes.

Linda Thompson

Almond Cake

4 eggs

3/4 cup sugar

1 tsp. baking powder

2 cups ground almonds

Preheat oven to 350 degrees.

Beat eggs and sugar until light and lemon-colored. Combine baking powder and nuts, and fold carefully into the egg mixture. Pour into a greased 9-inch springform pan. Bake 30 minutes. Cool in the pan. Remove to a plate and serve with whipped cream or ice cream.

Elaine Ashburn

Sweet Bread from Bjørkedal

1-2/3 cups milk

3 oz. yeast

3/4 cup butter

4 tbsps. sugar

2 eggs

4-3/4 cups flour

Vanilla cream: 1 package vanilla pudding mix (4 ounces)
                   1-2/3 cup whole milk
                   2 tbsps. sugar

Heat the milk to lukewarm and stir in the yeast. Melt the butter and add along with the sugar and eggs. Stir in half the flour, then knead in the rest. Cover with plastic wrap and let rise in a warm place.

Prepare the pudding according to the directions on the package, but with the lesser amount of milk and sugar.

Roll the dough into a rectangle. Spoon the vanilla pudding in the middle lengthwise. Fold the sides over the pudding. Shape into a big pretzel, seam side down. Snip with a scissors and pull the dough points in alternating directions.

Let rise. Preheat oven to 400 degrees. Bake 30 minutes.

Elaine Ashburn

Kvæfjord Cake
(The World's Best Dessert)

1/2 cup margarine (scant)

1/2 cup sugar

4 egg yolks

2/3 cup flour

1 tsp. baking powder

3-4 tbsps. milk

4 egg whites

1 cup sugar

3-1/2 tbsps. chopped almonds

1 package rum or vanilla pudding mix

1-1/4 cups whole milk

1-1/4 cups whipping cream

Preheat oven to 350 degrees.

Beat margarine and sugar until light and fluffy. Beat in the egg yolks, one at a time.

Sift the flour with the baking powder and add alternately with the milk.

Pour into a greased 9 x 13" pan.

Beat the egg whites until stiff, but not dry. Gradually add the sugar and beat until stiff and glossy. Spread over the cake batter. Sprinkle with almonds. Bake 20-25 minutes.

Cool, then cut in half lengthwise.

Prepare the pudding according to the package directions, but use only 1-1/4 cups milk. Cool. Whip the cream and fold into the pudding. Spread one cake layer with cream/pudding, then top with the other cake layer.

Elaine Ashburn

Whipped Cream Krumkake

1/2 cup butter, softened

1 cup sugar

1/2 tsp. nutmeg (or more to taste)

3 eggs

2 cups flour

1/2 cup whipping cream, whipped

In a mixing bowl, cream the butter. Add the sugar and eggs, then the nutmeg and flour.

In a separate bowl, whip the cream. Fold into the flour/sugar and egg mixture.

Heat the krumkake iron until hot. Lightly grease the iron to prevent sticking.

Drop about a teaspoon of dough in the center of the iron and close the iron. Squeeze it so that the dough is spread out thinly and evenly. Cook until light golden brown. There is no need to flip the flat krumkake. When golden brown, remove from iron and roll quickly on a cone shaped roller. This may be made of wood or metal. Leave on the roller with the seam side down. They cool and harden quickly, so by the time the next krumkake comes off the iron, the shape is set and the roller can be removed.

Store in a dry, cool place.

Krumkake can be filled with whipped cream or Cool Whip and topped with fruit. (We like to eat it plain).

Bonnie Eng

Buttermilk Krumkake

1 cup shortening (butter, margarine, crisco or combination)

1 cup sugar

2 eggs

1 tsp. vanilla

1 cup buttermilk

1 tsp. soda

2 cups flour

Cream sugar and shortening. Add eggs, beat well. Add vanilla. Sift flour and soda.

Add flour and buttermilk alternately.

Bake on krumkake iron until golden brown. Remove from iron and quickly shape on wooden cone roller. Set aside. Remove roller when cool.

Makes 3-4 dozen.

Note: This is a rather stiff batter.

Chuck Humphrey

Hard Tack

2 cups shortening or 1 cup butter and 1 cup Crisco

5 cups liquid: 2 cups milk, 3 cups water

3 tbsps. salt

1/2 cup sugar

2 cakes yeast

1 cup warm water

Approximately 12 cups of flour

Soak yeast in the 1 cup of warm water. Melt shortening with milk. Add salt, sugar, and the yeast mixture. Add enough flour until dough handles nicely. Knead until smooth. Let rise to double in bulk.

Shape dough into balls the size of large hamburger buns. Let rise again.

Roll each ball with a "knobby" rolling pin until very thin. Place onto cookie sheets.

Bake at 450 degrees until lightly browned.

Carolyn Holje

Kringle

1 cup sour cream

1 cup whipping cream

1 cup sugar

1 tsp. baking powder

1 tsp. soda

Mix all of the above, then add approximately 3-1/2 cups flour. Mix well.

To shape kringle, pinch off a piece of dough about the size of a small egg. Roll the dough with your hands to the thickness of a small cigar. Form into a wreath shape. Place on cookie sheet. Repeat with the remaining dough. Preheat oven to 400 degrees. Bake on lower rack for 4 minutes, then upper rack for 4 minutes. Remove from cookie sheet and place in a bowl. Cover with a flour sack towel until cool. The kringle freeze beautifully.

Louise Tjernagel

Sandbakkels

1/2 cup butter

1/2 cup sugar

1 small egg, unbeaten

1 tsp. almond extract

1-1/2 cups flour

Cream butter. Add sugar and mix very well. Add egg, almond extract, and enough flour to make a stiff dough. Chill slightly.

Shape into sandbakkel tins.

Place on cookie sheet and bake at 375 degrees for 10 minutes.

Remove from oven. Allow to cool. Gently pinch tins to remove.

Makes 50 small sandbakkels.

John Tjernagel

Sweet Soup

Note: This is all very approximate and can vary according to your preference.

1-2 apples, peeled

1 orange peeled or 1 small can mandarin oranges

1 15 oz. can each: peaches, apricots, pears

1/2 lb. prunes, cooked and pureed

1/2 cup raisins or craisins

Dice all fruit

1/2 cup dry pearl tapioca or scant 1/2 cup minute tapioca

Soak pearl tapioca 12 to 24 hours. Simmer in soaking water and juice until all pearls are clear or almost clear. They will continue "clearing" as it sits and cools.

Juice—liquid from fruits plus any combination of apple, pineapple, orange juice to make approximately 4-6 cups total to right consistency.

Add diced fruit and juice. Don't add all juice right away; wait to see how thick the tapioca makes it. Simmer to have flavors blend.

Sugar to taste (which will depend on juices used).

2 sticks cinnamon or 1 tsp. ground cinnamon

1/4 tsp. salt

Suzanne Asplin, Bonita Garthus

Oslo Kringla

1/2 cup butter

1 cup boiling water

1 cup flour

1 tsp. almond extract

3 eggs

Melt butter in boiling water. Add flour and almond extract. Add eggs one at a time, beating well after each. Let cool. While cooling, make:

Bottom Crust

1/2 cup butter

1 cup flour

1 tbsp. water

A few drops of almond flavoring

Mix as for pie crust.

Pat into 2 rectangles, about 3 x 13 inches, side by side on a cookie sheet, but not touching, OR make one large rectangle.

Spread cooled mixture over crusts and bake at 375 degrees for 45 minutes.

Frost while warm with powdered sugar frosting flavored with almond. Sprinkle slivered almonds on top.

To serve, cut in strips.

Karen Humphrey

Norwegian Waffles

2 eggs

2 tbsps. sugar

1/4 tsp. salt

1-1/2 cups flour

1-1/2 cups regular milk

1/2 cup buttermilk

3 tbsps. melted butter or margarine

Cardamom to taste (at least 1 tbsp.)

Mix eggs and sugar well. Mix in salt and milk. Then, little by little stir in flour. (Be sure it does not get lumpy.) Melt butter and stir that into the batter. Add cardamom. Let the batter stand at room temperature for approximately one hour.

Warm up the waffle iron (should not need to be buttered) and fry the waffles until golden brown. Stack waffles on top of each other so they stay warm and soft.

Serve with sour cream, whipped cream, any preserves, fresh berries, butter and sugar, or whatever your heart desires.

Kjell Nordlie

Rømmegrøt

4 cups fresh cream (directly from the farm)

3/4 cup sifted flour

4 cups boiling whole milk

Dash of salt

Sugar and cinnamon

Allow cream to stand in refrigerator for a week before using.

Put cream on low heat and bring to a boil. After boiling point is reached, boil 20 minutes, stirring occasionally. Add sifted flour gradually, stirring constantly. Butterfat will separate and come to the top. Continue to stir and skim off the butterfat. Set aside.

Stir boiled milk into the cream/flour mixture, blending until smooth and glossy. Add salt. Blend again.

Serve rømmegrøt in small, individual dessert dishes. Pour the butterfat on top and sprinkle with sugar and cinnamon. Best served warm. Melted butter may be used in place of the butterfat.

Serves 12-20.

Ronette Doering and Karen Humphrey

Ost Kaka

1 gallon fresh cow's milk
1 cup flour
1/2 rennet tablet
1 tbsp. cool water
3 eggs, beaten
1 cup heavy cream
1/2 cup sugar
1/2 tsp. almond extract

Pour milk in a 6-quart pan and let sit two days in the refrigerator, then let set at room temperature overnight.

Dissolve the 1/2 rennet tablet in 1 tbsp. cool water.

Sift flour into the warm milk and mix well.

Add the water/rennet tablet mixture.

Let set until firm. (Time to firm up depends on the room temperature or the condition of the milk. Sometimes it takes one hour or longer. If it doesn't make a firm curd in two hours, add another 1/2 rennet tablet dissolved in water. Once it is firm, draw a knife through it a few times to start the separation of curd and whey.)

Stir up, drain off whey.* Put curds in a 2-quart bowl.

Add the cream, sugar, eggs. Beat with hand mixer until combined. Sprinkle with nutmeg.

Bake at 325 degrees one hour or until well done. The top will be browned. Some whey may appear in the center or around edges.

To serve, spoon ost kaka in a dessert dish, with a little cream poured over it, or topped with lingonberry, strawberry, or raspberry sauce.

Elaine Ashburn

Elaine freezes the whey and uses it in bread dough.

Christmas Wreath Cookies

1/4 lb. (one stick) butter

10.5 oz. package of miniature marshmallows

8-1/2 cups corn flakes

1/2 tsp. vanilla extract

1 tsp. green food coloring

Red hot cinnamon candles

Melt butter slowly. Add marshmallow to melted butter. Melt marshmallows slowly; then add vanilla and green food coloring. When mixture is consistent "goo," gradually add corn flakes in two batches, taking care to cover flakes with the green mixture and taking care not to overdo the stirring so as to break cornflakes into small pieces. Form into wreath shapes and decorate with three red cinnamon candies while mixture is still warm.

Note: It can help to butter your hands before shaping wreaths, as the mixture is sticky. You can also use a scoop or large cooking spoon to drop the mixture onto waxed paper (taped down to counter), then use your index finger to make a hole in the middle while pressing the rest of the mixture into a wreath shape. You also can make one large wreath and then cut it into individual servings.

Lorayne Pitchford (Jensen)

For a Smørgasbord Table

Norwegian Potato Salad

Boil 3-5 pounds of small new red potatoes with skins on until tender/firm.

Cool and cut into bite size pieces. Do not remove skins.

Chop fine 6 green onions, including green tops.

1 tbsp. finely chopped fresh dill. (Dry dill weed can be used, but use less.)

Dressing:

2 cups sour cream (or potato topping with chive and onion is very good)

1 cup Miracle Whip

1/2 to 1 tsp. sugar to taste

Salt to taste

Toss potatoes with dressing. Best if allowed to rest approximately 1 hour before serving.

Howard Amundson

Cabbage Casserole

1 pound ground beef, browned

1 medium head of cabbage, shredded

1 medium onion, chopped

Toss together and place in casserole.

Pour 1 can Campbell's cream of tomato soup over cabbage mixture.

Add 1 tsp. salt.

Cover and bake in oven at 325 degrees until cabbage is tender. Stir at least once during baking. If cabbage gets dry, add small amount of water.

Howard Amundson

Meatballs in Gravy

1 lb. ground beef

1/2 lb. ground pork

1/2 cup dry bread crumbs

1 medium potato, cooked and mashed

1 onion, peeled and ground fine

1 tsp. ground ginger

1 tsp. salt

1/8 tsp. pepper

3 tbsp. fat for browning

2 cups beef broth

1 tbsp. flour

Mix all ingredients, except fat, liquids, and flour, as for meat loaf. Form into small balls and brown in heavy frying pan which has a lid. Remove balls, reduce heat, and add broth to frying pan. Thicken with flour which has been mixed to a smooth paste with a little cold water to make a thin gravy. Put meatballs back in the gravy, cover and simmer one hour.

Serve with mashed potatoes.

Note: Hot tomato juice can be added to the gravy for flavor or consistency if desired.

These meatballs are very good warmed up the second day.

Leatrice Nielsen

Dave's Refrigerator Pickles

7 cups sliced cucumbers (unpeeled)

1 medium yellow onion, sliced

Mix in bowl:

1 cup vinegar

2 tbsps. canning salt

1-1/2 cups sugar

Pour mixed ingredients over cucumber and onion.

Put in jars or covered tupperware and refrigerate.

Add a little dill if you like.

Dave Guennigsman

Chunky Salsa, Homemade (D'Salsa)

4 big red tomatoes

1 green pepper

1 yellow or red pepper

1 medium onion (red or yellow)

Ground black pepper

Lawry's seasoned salt

Garlic salt with parsley

Ortega Taco Sauce (mild)

Dice tomatoes and drain off excess water. Dice peppers
and onion and combine with tomatoes. Lightly add ground
black pepper, Lawry's, and garlic salt. Add about 12oz.
taco sauce. Stir together. Add more seasoning to taste.

This will keep for a week in the refrigerator.

*Note: if you like it hot, you can use hot peppers and hot taco
sauce.*

Dave Guennigsman

Grilled Salmon or Trout

Salmon or trout fillet

Sea salt (not regular salt)

2 tbsps. butter

Fresh dill

Aluminum foil

Cut aluminum foil so it is big enough to wrap the fillet without it leaking.

Put 1 tbsp. butter on the foil where the fillet will be lying and sprinkle some sea salt and dill on the same area. Lay the fillet on top of the dill and sea salt. Put 1 tbsp. butter, sea salt, and dill on fillet. Wrap the fish in foil.

Heat grill to approximately 450 degrees. Put wrapped fish on grill and cook for seven minutes. Turn the package over and cook for another seven minutes.

Unwrap fish, and it is ready to serve.

Enjoy with boiled potatoes, fresh asparagus, bérnaise sauce, and refrigerated pickles.

Kjell Nordlie

Grandpa Bob's Baked Beans

1 can baked beans (with sauce)

1 can white (navy) beans, drained

1 can pinto beans, drained

4 tbsps. dark molasses

4 tbsps. Worcestershire sauce

2 tbsps. yellow mustard

4 tbsps. catsup

4 tbsps. barbeque sauce

2 tbsps. red hot sauce (optional)

4 cloves garlic (optional)

1 green pepper, chopped into 1/4 inch pieces

1 red pepper, chopped into 1/4 inch pieces

1/2 of a 3 inch onion, finely chopped

4 strips thick bacon, sliced into 1" pieces

2 Andouille sausages, sliced into 1/8 inch slices (or other sausage)

Chop all the vegetables and pour into 9 x 13" casserole dish.

Add beans and spices and mix.

Fry the sausages and bacon to get most of the fat out, then add to casserole

Mix, then bake at 350 degrees for 2 hours (until most of the liquid has been evaporated). Top should be browned nicely.

Mechele Pitchford

Grape Salad

2 lbs. seedless green grapes

2 lbs. seedless red grapes

8 oz. package cream cheese, softened

1/2 cup white sugar

8 oz. carton sour cream

1 cup chopped pecans

3/4 cup brown sugar

Rinse grapes and dry thoroughly. In a large bowl, beat together the cream cheese, sugar, sour cream, and vanilla. Fold in grapes; mix until evenly distributed.

Place in a flat container, such as a 9 x 13" cake pan.

Sprinkle pecans and brown sugar over top. Chill at least three hours before serving.

Tim and Helen Kringle

Lutefisk

3 lbs. lutefisk

1 tbsp. salt

Boil about one gallon of water with salt added in a large kettle. Add lutefisk. When water returns to a boil, remove fish. Keep warm in a colander over (not in) hot water. Serve with melted butter (if you are Norwegian) or cream sauce (if you are Swedish).

Anonymous

Modern Day Lefse

1/4 lb. butter

1 cup plus 2 tbsps. water

1 tbsp. sugar

2-2/3 cups potato flakes

1-1/2 tsps. salt

1-1/3 cups whole milk

Heat together the butter, water, salt, and sugar. Stir in the flakes. Mix well. Add the cold milk. Mix well. Cover and refrigerate overnight.

The next day, work 1 cup plus 3 tbsps. flour into potato mixture. Divide into 16 pieces.

Heat lefse iron to 450-500 degrees F.

Using a well floured stocking-covered rolling pin, roll each piece of dough on a floured board or cloth until quite thin. Use a lefse turning stick to slide under the lefse and start to roll it on the stick. Transfer to the lefse iron. Fry until lightly browned. The edges will brown first, and there may be bubbles that erupt. Pop them. Flip the lefse with the turning stick and fry the other side. When done, remove the lefse from the griddle with the lefse stick and tuck them between two pieces of wax paper that are inside a tablecloth. This keeps them warm and moist.

Serve with butter and sugar or sugar and cinnamon as desired.

Makes 16 whole lefse.

Bonnie Eng

Swedish Rye Bread

2 packages dry yeast

1 quart lukewarm water

1 tsp. white sugar

8-9 cups white bread flour, divided (1 cup for sponge, about 6-7 cups for dough, remaining flour for kneading)

1/4 cup molasses

1 pinch soda (about 1/4 tsp.)

1/4 cup melted shortening

1 cup brown sugar

1 tsp. anise seed, if desired

1 tsp. salt

3 cups medium rye flour

Dissolve yeast in lukewarm water to which the 1 tsp. sugar has been added. Add about 1 cup white flour (enough to make a soft sponge) and let stand in warm place until bubbly, about 10 minutes. Warm molasses; add pinch of soda. Add the molasses and the melted shortening to the sponge. Then add brown sugar, salt, rye flour, and anise, beating well. Gradually add about 7 cups white flour (enough to make a stiff dough). Knead on lightly floured board until smooth. Put into greased bowl, cover with towel, and set in warm place to rise. When doubled in bulk (about 2 hours), knead on floured board, return to bowl and let rise again (about 1 hour). When light, shape into loaves, place in greased bread pans, and let rise again. Bake in moderate oven (350-375 degrees) about 45 minutes.

Note: Instead of putting into regular sized loaf pans, you can use a smaller sized loaf pan and make seven loaves from this recipe. The baking time will be shorter.

Earl Doering

Modern Day Rømmegrøt

Made with homogenized milk and cream from the store. The butter does not separate out as in the original recipe, so is added to the milk and also poured on top. Some people serve it from a crock pot with thinly sliced butter on top, letting the butter melt in the pot.

2 sticks butter

3/4 cup sifted flour

1 quart whole milk

1 pint half-and-half*

1/2 cup to 3/4 cup sugar

Melt 1 stick butter at low to medium temperature. Add flour gradually. Slowly bring to a boil, stirring constantly. While butter melts, heat milk and half-and-half to a boil over low heat; gradually add to the flour mixture. Let cook, stirring constantly, until it thickens. Add sugar to taste, stir until smooth and glossy.

Melt second stick of butter for the top, if desired, and serve with cinnamon and sugar.

If desired, substitute sour cream for the half-and-half to give taste closer to the original.

Ronette Doering and Karen Humphrey

Swedish Fruit Soup (Frukt Soppa)

Soak in water to cover overnight:

1 (12 oz) pkg. mixed dried fruit

1/2 cup raisins

1 orange, sliced (with rind)

1 lemon, sliced (with rind)

1 cup sugar

1/4 cup tapioca

1 stick cinnamon

Add the next day:

3 apples, peeled, cored, and diced

1 tbsp. vinegar

Cook over low heat until fruit is soft (30-45 minutes), stirring occasionally.

Serve hot or cold. Can be served over ice cream, if you like.

Ronette Doering

Traditional Lefse

4 cups riced potatoes

1/4 cup butter

1/4 cup margarine

1 tsp. sugar

1/4 cup milk

Mix all together, cover, and refrigerate overnight.

When ready to roll lefse, add:

1-1/4 cups – 1-1/2 cups flour

1/2 tsp. baking powder

pinch of salt

Mix together well. Roll out with lefse rolling pin on floured cloth until very thin.

Bake on very hot griddle until bubbles form. Turn to the other side until lightly browned.

Makes about one dozen whole lefse.

Chuck and Karen Humphrey

Remembering the Good Times . . . and There Are Many!

A key part of the Dassel Leikarring all through their thirty-year history is the sociability of the group. Birthdays, wedding anniversaries, Super Bowl Sundays, and Memorial Day weekends, the Leikarring members have celebrated each other's happiness, and divided each other's grief. "There have been great parties and much laughter," Lois Weeks recounted.

- Elaine pretended that she had eaten poison berries thinking they were lingonberries. She put a white ring of make-up around her lips and told Kjell that she was feeling strange. Unfortunately we couldn't keep the laughter at bay very long. But then again, laughter was never long in coming with the Leikarring!

- Jim Weeks accidentally dumped a canvas load of water down Ronette's neck while on the pontoon boat.

- A video tape of the Leikarring dance performance in Lindsborg, Kansas, revealed some choice words by visiting dancers from Omaha: "They are sure good dancers but they really need to work on their bows."

- Lindsborg, Kansas, 1995: In the most Swedish town in America, dancing in the Swedish Pavilion from the 1904 Saint Louis World's Fair with a host of Swedish folk dancers from Lindsborg, Omaha, and Kansas City, the lone true Norwegian, Kjell Nordlie, and the Dassel

Leikarring teach all the Swedes how to do the Stockholm Schottische.

- The Dassel Leikarring is a social group that enjoys each other's company. It was the Pitchford's turn to host a party. Feeling shy about not hosting sooner, Mechele announced at a dance practice, "I would have people over more often but we have no ice." Her intent was to convey that the ice maker in their refrigerator did not work, so she was reluctant to have guests over. On the night of the party, as the door bell rang, each dancer at the door cheerfully greeted her saying, "Oh, I heard you needed some ice." Each guest snickered as they deposited multiple ten-pound bags of ice outside on the porch. By the time all the dancers arrived the ice pile had grown into a small glacier. "It still makes us laugh and smile," Mechele said, "about my excuse for not having friends over: no ice."

- In the early days, we'd meet at someone's house before driving to a performance, and at whose ever house we met there were coffee and cookies for those who came early. Occasionally someone would remark, "Do we have to go dancing? Couldn't we just stay right here and talk?" There was such a good sense of fellowship, and good food.

- It was really something to have the mayor of our town be such a supporter of the Leikarring that he and his wife would go with us to the performances.

- David Borg once wore his knickers backwards.

- Kjell once needed an immediate knickers repair! The dance, Sandsværril, has since been known as the "rip the pants dance."

- Dancing for parents' wedding anniversaries and landmark birthdays and at church anniversaries has been memorable.

- The Nordlies went to the 1994 Winter Olympics in Lillehammer. Many of us, very proud that Norway was hosting the Olympics, watched every possible moment of the broadcasts, glued to our televisions. And one morning, on the NBC *Today Show,* we saw the Nordlies waving to all their friends back home!

- Impromptu dancing in a Duluth hotel lobby was accompanied by the famous American Hardanger fiddler, Loretta Kelly, who was staying in the same hotel.

- Impromptu dancing occurred in the Schipol airport in Amsterdam when the flight the Nordlies, the Doerings, and the Humphreys were taking home was delayed twelve hours.

- Impromptu dancing took place in a small town in Holland by the Nordlies and the Doerings when the Humphreys had to return to the previous night's hotel for a bag they had forgotten.

- Impromptu dancing occurred at the Main Street Hotel, Sauk Center, by the Doerings and the Humphreys where they were stranded in a March blizzard.

The Leikarring has never forgotten their founding on New Year's Eve 1981. They gather every year to celebrate. Sometimes they have booked hotel rooms together so they and their children could swim in the hotel pool, go to a restaurant, and enjoy the luxury of sleeping in on New Year's Day. More often than not, the Leikarring has gathered at someone's home for a potluck supper or a planned supper. Occasionally there have been murder mysteries that the group has acted, or there are card games, or charades, or songs that people have made for the occasion and are performed. At the turn of the millennium, the Nordlies hosted everyone with a gala dinner. The centerpiece was a standing rib roast with spritzing sparklers that added to the gaiety. For that occasion, there were champagne flutes, crowns, and jewelry to commemorate the landmark event.

The thirtieth anniversary of the Leikarring, however, was celebrated with a reunion in August 2011, at the Dassel History Center. The dining area was decorated with several Norwegian and Swedish items brought from homes for the occasion, and there were several displays of photographs taken over the thirty years. The evening began with a grand Grand March led by Kjell and Elaine with music provided by Ron Nelson. Before a delicious catered buffet dinner, the table grace was sung in Norwegian:

I Jesu navn går vi til bords

Å spise drikke på ditt ord;

Deg Gud til ære os til gavn

Så får vi mat i Jesu navn.

Amen.

The Leikarring sang as a wonderful choir, in four-part harmony. Place cards were beautifully crafted programs with rosemaling and a list of all the dancers from 1981-2011. The programs were tied with ribbons in the colors of the Norwegian flag—blue, white, and red.

During the program, with Cliff Eng acting as master of ceremonies, greetings and stories were shared with each other, then movies from the oldest days of the Leikarring were viewed on the "big screen." How good everyone thought they looked! How well they danced! Some commented, "We were so young!" There were movies of the children of the Leikarring, many of whom are now married with children of their own. A moment of silence was held to honor the memory of Willie Carlson and Ewald Nielsen who had died.

Kjell and Elaine expressed appreciation to everyone, and in turn, the dancers expressed gratitude to two marvelous people who gave them the joy of dancing. And following the program, the dancing continued!

Kjell & Elaine Nordlie

Endnotes

1   For further information on the history and revival of Norwegian folk dance see Johan Krogsæter, *Folk Dancing in Norway*, trans. Brenda Koren, (Oslo: Tanum-Norli, 1968); Klara Semb, *Dances of Norway* (London: Max Parrish and Co. Limited, 1951).

2   June Drennings Holmquist, ed. *They Chose Minnesota: A Survey of the State's Ethnic Groups* (St. Paul: Minnesota Historical Society Press, 1981).

3   The runic inscription has been translated to read: "We are eight Goths and twenty-two Norwegians on an exploration journey from Vinland through the West. We had camp by a lake with two skerries one day's journey north from this stone. We were out and fished one day. After we came home, we found ten of our men red with blood and dead. AVM save us from evil. We have ten of our party by the sea to look after our ships, fourteen days' journey from this island. Year 1362."

4   Dr. Emeroy Johnson, "Was Oza Windib a Swede?" *The Swedish-American Historical Quarterly*, July 1984.

5   Holmquist.

6   Fredrika Bremer, *Homes of the New World* (New York: Harper & Brothers, 1853).

7   Father Pierz, quoted in *Worship and Work: St. John's Abbey & University 1856-1956*, Father Coleman Barry (Collegeville, Minnesota: Order of St. Benedict, 1956).

8   Author interview with Richard Coleman, Dassel, November 1982.

9   Oscar Lindquist, *Dassel, Minnesota: Those Were the Days, 1869-1904*. (Dassel: The Dassel Dispatch, 1943).

10 Ahnfelt also set the poems of Lina Sandell-Berg to music, among them "Day by Day."

11 Lindquist.

12 Andrew Volstead really wanted to be remembered for being the

author of the Cooperative Marketing Act, also known as the Capper-Volstead Act, which passed in 1922 and enabled farmers to organize marketing and producer cooperatives on a stock basis. Cooperatives were also an important economic factor in Dassel-Cokato.

13 Syttende Mai commemorates the signing of the constitution at Eidsvoll, May 17, 1804, declaring Norway to be an independent nation. The national holiday is unique among such celebrations because the day consists of children's parades in every community, with bands, ice cream, and candy for the children, and folk dancing. This national holiday is one without a display of military might.

14 Per, the fiddler, had only one cow, He traded his cow and got his fiddle back. You old good fiddle, you fiddle, you fiddle of mine. Per, the fiddler played and the fiddle made such music that the boys danced and the girls cried. You old good fiddle, you fiddle, you fiddle of mine!

15 Author interview with Ellen Tofteberg, Råde, Norway, June 1997.

16 *Dassel Dispatch (May 13, 1982).*

17 Hauling water, hauling wood, hauling lumber over the hill.

18 Author interview with David and Sharon Borg, April 1997.

19 Author interview with John and Louise Tjernagel, April 1997.

20 Author interview with Dennis and Elaine Ashburn, April 1997.

21 Kjersti Skavhaug, *Norwegian Bunads* (Oslo: Hjemmenes Forlag, 1982). English edition by Bent Vanberg.

22 For a schedule of the Leikarring's performances, see Appendix B.

23 For a list of Leikarring members since 1981, see Appendix C.

24 The small building, shaped very-much like a mushroom, was built to be a gas station. It is situated on the corner of Highway 12 and First Street North.

25 For a list of the more than fifty dances performed by the Leikarring, see Appendix A.

26 See Appendix E for genealogy of some Leikarring members.

27 Author interview with Ronette Doering, 2012.

28 Eva Valebrokk and Thomas Thiis-Evensen, Norway's Stave Churches: Architecture, History, and Legends, trans. Ann Clay Zwick (Oslo: Boksenteret, 1994).

29 Klara Semb, *Dances of Norway* (London: Max Parrish & Company, 1951).

30 Semb.

Photos

**The Dassel and Råde Leikarrings
in front of Bøndernes Hus in Råde, Norway 1985.**

Front row: Vigdis Fjelle (Berg), Grete Tofteberg (Weel), Ingjerd Berg, Hilde Holmen.

Second Row: Kari Lisbeth Hovland, Grethe Tollefsrød, Reidun Sørlie, Turid Solgaard, Elaine Nordlie, Ronette Doering, Kate Sørensen, Karen Humphrey.

Third row: Engebreth Tofteberg, Johannes Kirkerød, Chuck Humphrey, Kjell Olav Nordlie, Vidar Sørlie, Per auberg, Kjell Løkke, Ron Nelson, Ole Johan Holmen, Knut Berg, Per Hvidsen, Earl Doering.

Rotary Lutefisk Dinner
Dassel-Cokato High School, December 1986

Ron Nelson, accordian.

Front Row: Mark Borg, Karna Humphrey, Tim Borg. Second Row: Chuck Humphrey, John Tjernagel, Craig Holje, Kjell Nordlie, Earl Doering, David Borg, Dan Holje. Third Row: Karen Humphrey, Louise Tjernagel, Catherine Nordlie, Elaine Nordlie, Ronette Doering, Sharon Borg, Carolyn Holje.

**Iron World
Chisholm, 1994**

Kneeling: Willie Carlson, Dennis Ashburn, Kjell Nordlie, Earl Doering, Chuck Humphrey, Jon Petter Olsen, John Tjernagel.

Standing: Joyce Carlson, Elaine Ashburn, Elaine Nordlie, Ronette Doering, Karen Humphrey, Louise Tjernagel, Anne Enger.

Olsen and Enger were visiting from the Råde Leikarring.

Little Mountain Settlement
Monticello, 2001

Seated: Heidi Guenningsman, Elaine Nordlie, Elaine Ashburn, Ronette Doering.

Standing: Dave Guenningsman, Kjell Nordlie, Dennis Ashburn, Earl Doering, Howard Amundson, David Pitchford, Marlene Amundson, Mechele Pitchford.

Moose Lake
2004

Front Row: Heidi Guenningsman, Lois Weeks, Elaine Nordlie, Mechelle Pitchford, Leatrice Nielsen, Ronette Doering, Elaine Ashburn, Sandy Dopkins.

Second Row: Dave Guenningsman, Jim Weeks, Kjell Nordlie, David Pitchford, Ewald Nielsen, Earl Doering, Denis Ashburn, Bob Dopkins.

Milan Syttende Mai Festival
2006

Front Row: Heidi Guenningsman, Leatrice Nielsen, Sandy Dopkins, Ronette Doering, Elaine Nordlie, Bonnie Eng, Mehele Pitchford, Marlene Amundson.

Second Row: Dave Guenningsman, Ewald Nielsen, Bob Dopkins, Earl Doering, Cliff Eng, David Pitchford, Howard Amundson, Kjell Nordlie, Dennnis Ashburn.

Mora
2010

Kneeling: David Guenningsman, David Thompson, Dennis Ashburn, Kjell Nordlie, Clint Lindquist, David Pitchford, Earl Doering.

Standing: Heidi Guenningsman, Linda Thompson, Elaine Ashburn, Elaine Nordlie, Ronette Doering, Brenda Lindquist, Bonita Garthus, Mechele Pitchford, Su Asplin, Leatrice Nielsen.

Dances of the Dassel Leikarring

DANCE	ORIGIN	NUMBER OF DANCERS	DIFFICULTY
Couple Dances:			
Telespringar	Norway	Many	Advanced
Teleganger	Norway	Many	Intermediate
Østfoldspringar	Norway	Many	Advanced
Icelandic Schottische	Iceland	Many	Intermediate
Stretch-pants Polka	Norway	Many	Easy
Råde Waltz	Norway	Many	Easy
Hambo	Sweden	Many	Advanced
Mazurka	Sweden	Many	Advanced
Rørospols	Norway	Many	Advanced
Song Dances:			
Per Spelmann	Norway	Many	Easy
Å Kjøre Vatten	Norway	Many	Intermediate
Å Eg Ser På Deg	Norway	Many	Intermediate
Å Vesle Kari Vår	Norway	Many	Intermediate
Bendik og Årolilja	Norway	Many	Intermediate
Fram Dansar Ein Haugkall	Norway	Many	Intermediate

Mixers:

Trans-Atlantic Mixer		Many	Intermediate
Familievals	Denmark	Many	Easy
Stockholm-Schottische	Sweden	Many	Intermediate
Four-step mixer	Sweden	Many	Easy

Turdanser:

Eikerril	Norway (Vestfossen, Eiker)	6 couples	Advanced
Holt-ril	Norway (Holt, Aust-Agder)	3 couples	Advanced
Ril fra Donna	Norway	2 couples	Intermediate
Sandsværril	Norway (Buskerud)	6-8 couples	Intermediate
Seksmannsril	Norway (Asker)	3 couples	Intermediate
Feiar fra Vestlandet	Norway	6-8 couples	Advanced
Feiar med Vals (Sweeper)	Norway (Ringerike)	Many couples	Intermediate
Åttetur med Mylne (Millwheel)	Norway	4-6 couples	Intermediate
Toppede Høne (Crested Hen)	Denmark	4 couples	Intermediate
Krossdans med Seks	Norway (Sogn)	2 men, 4 women	Intermediate
Klappdans (Clappdance)	Norway	Many couples	Easy
Jamstpolska	Sweden	3 or 6 couples	Advanced
Pariserpolka	Norway	Many couples	Intermediate
Gamal Reinlender	Norway	Many couples	Advanced
Snuspolka	Norway	Many couples	Intermediate
Lirpu Larpu (Limpy Larsen)	Finnish	Many couples	Advanced

Firetur fra Landvik	Norway	Many couples	Advanced
Sjynmyrvals	Denmark	Many couples	Easy
Rugen	Norway	Many couples	Easy
Gilleråsen (Twelve-step)	Norway (Gjemnes, Nordmøre)	3 couples	Easy
Sekstur I fra Namdalen	Norway (Namdale)	Many couples	Advanced
Veva-vadmæl (Weaving Dance)	Sweden	Many couples	Advanced
Tretur fra Fana (Greetdance)	Norway	12 people	Easy
Kvadrilje	Norway	4 couples	Advanced
Oksedansen	Sweden	2 men	Intermediate
Telespringar for tre (Telemark)	Norway	1 man, 2 women	Intermediate
Telespringar (Telemark)	Norway	Couples	Advanced
Telegangar (Telemark)	Norway	Couples	Advanced
Tretur fra Hordaland (Flirtdance)	Norway (Hordaland)	1 man, 2 women	Intermediate
Firetur fra Nes	Norway	2 couples	Intermediate
Totur fra Holt	Norway	2 couples	Advanced
Moelledansen	Norway	8 couples	Advanced
Attepardansen	Norway	8 couples	Intermediate
Stjernedans (Østfold)	Norway	4 couples	Advanced

Performances of the Dassel Leikarring
(Incomplete Listing)

1982 – Performances

May 15	Litchfield, Minnesota – National Guard Armory Syttende Mai Celebration
September	Dassel, Minnesota – Ball Park Red Rooster Days

1984 – Performances

May 15	Litchfield, Minnesota Sons of Norway Syttende Mai Celebration
May 17	Hudson, Wisconsin – Hudson House Inn St. Croix Valley Syttende Mai Society
May	Dassel, Minnesota – Home of Helen & Walter Johnson for their Fiftieth Wedding Anniversary
July 4	Spicer, Minnesota July 4th Parade (We danced on a flatbed.)
August 4	Chisholm, Minnesota – Iron Range Interpretative Center Scandinavian Day
August	Dassel, Minnesota Lakeside Nursing Home
September	Dassel, Minnesota Red Rooster Day Celebration
October 16	Hutchinson, Minnesota – Crow River Golf Club Ladies Fall Dinner
November 10	Brooten, Minnesota – High School Ethnic Holiday

December	Dassel, Minnesota – D.C. High School Lutefisk Supper

1985 – Performances

January 12	Cokato, Minnesota – Cokato Elementary School Queen Carnival
February 9	Hutchinson, Minnesota – High School Winter Carnival
February 10	Darwin, Minnesota – Catholic Church Renewal of Wedding Vows
April 30	Litchfield, Minnesota – High School Gym Home-Extension Spring Banquet
May 3	St. Paul, Minnesota – Civic Center Festival of Nations
May 18	Sunberg, Minnesota – on the street Syttende Mai Celebration
May 21	St. Cloud, Minnesota St. Cloud University Atwood Center Sons of Norway Trollheim Lodge
May 28	**June Trip to Norway** Participated in Østfold Springer Competition (Doerings, Humphreys, Nelsons, and Nordlies)
June 30	Starbuck, Minnesota – Park Norwegian Celebration
July 14	Norseland, Minnesota – Annexstad Farm Wedding Reception
August 11	Esterville, Iowa – Church Geneva & Walamar Fransdal's 50th Wedding Anniversary
September 19	Glencoe, Minnesota – Courthouse Basement Home Extension Kick-Off
September 22	Minneapolis, Minnesota – Radisson South Opening of the Kaffestova
November 19	Willmar, Minnesota – Willmar Health Care Center
December 7	Cokato, Minnesota – D.C. High School Lutefisk Supper
December 10	Dassel, Minnesota – Senior Citizen's Apartments Potluck of the Month

1986 – Performances

March 8	Brainerd, Minnesota – Senior High School Heritage Fest
May 17	Litchfield, Minnesota – Emmaus Nursing Home
June 10	Dassel, Minnesota – Dassel Lakeside Home
June 14	Kerkhoven, Minnesota – Park Western Days
June 21	Renville, Minnesota – First Lutheran Church 10th Anniversary, Scandinavian Midsummer Fest
June 22	Glenwood, Minnesota – Park Sons of Norway Midsummer Fest
July 11-13	Chisholm, Minnesota – Iron World Ethnic Festival
July 24-25	**Swedes from Dalarne come** Dassel, Minnesota – High School
August 9	Rake, Iowa – Main Street Mange Takk Days
September	Edina, Minnesota Radisson South
	Hutchinson, Minnesota – Mall Heritage Festival

1987 – Performances

June 4	Minneapolis, Minnesota – Radisson at Ridgedale Farmers' Broadcasting Convention
June	**Trip to Norway**
June 13	Østfold Springer Competition (Borgs, Doerings, Humphreys, and Nordlies)
July 24-26	Decorah, Iowa – Street (all three days) 21st Annual Nordic Fest Jasper, Minnesota
September 13	Minneapolis, Minnesota – Radisson South
December 5	Cokato, Minnesota – D.C. High School Lutefisk Supper
December 12	Lakeville, Minnesota Sons of Norway Christmas Party

1988 – Performances

March 19	Brainerd, Minnesota – Senior High School Heritage Fest
April 19	Cokato, Minnesota – Baptist Church District Federated Women's Club
April 30	Grove City, Minnesota Community Center Brunch
May 14	Minneapolis, Minnesota – Peavey Plaza Parade Syttende Mai Celebration
May 21	Lakeville, Minnesota – Norsota Lodge Mock Norwegian Country Wedding
May 28-June 2	**Råde Leikarring visits us**
May 30	Dassel, Minnesota – Dassel Elementary School Gym Råde Leikarring & Dassel Leikarring Perform
June 1	Montevideo, Minnesota – Pioneer Village Råde Leikarring & Dassel Leikarrings Perform
June 19	Minneapolis, Minnesota – Hyland Park, Bloomington Midsummer: Minnesota Festival of Music with a Swedish Wedding

1989 – Performances

May 11	St. Cloud, Minnesota – Crossroads Shopping Center Senior Expo
May 19	Minneapolis, Minnesota Sons of Norway Headquarters Norumberga Lodge's Syttende Mai Celebration
May 20	Milan, Minnesota Syttende Mai Celebration
June 24	Fargo, North Dakota – Trollwood Park Twelfth Annual Scandinavian Hjemkomst Festival
October	Minneapolis, Minnesota – Brooklyn Center Mall Sons of Norway Nidaros Lodge

1990 – Performances

May 20	Monticello, Minnesota – Little Mountain Settlement
June 24	Fargo, North Dakota – Trollwood Park Thirteenth Annual Scandinavian Hjemkomst Festival

June 25	Dawson, Minnesota – Providence Church
	St. Cloud, Minnesota – Sunwood Inn Vestlandslaget Stevne
July 18-21	New Ulm, Minnesota Heritage Fest at the Holiday Inn

1991 – Performances

May 16	Milan, Minnesota Syttende Mai Celebration
June 6-8	Northfield, Minnesota – St. Olaf College Vestlandslaget Stevne
June 23	Minneapolis, Minnesota – Minnehaha Park Svenskernas Dag
June 27-28	Fargo, North Dakota – Trollwood Park and Civic Auditorium – Fourteenth Annual Scandinavian Hjemomst Festival
October 6	St. Joseph (St. Cloud) – St. Benedict's Center Oktoberfest "Celebration of Nations"

1992 – Performances

March 14	Brainerd, Minnesota – High School
April 23	St. Cloud, Minnesota – Senior Citizen Center Sons of Norway Trollheim Lodge
May 15	Minneapolis, Minnesota – Swedish Institute Sons of Norway
May 16	Milan, Minnesota – on Main Street Syttende Mai Celebration
July 11	Chisholm, Minnesota – Iron Range Interpretive Center Scandinavian Day
	Northfield, Minnesota St. Olaf College – Lag Annual Meeting

1993 – Performances

May 23	Monticello, Minnesota – Little Mountain Settlement
June 26	Montevideo, Minnesota – Trøndelag Lodge
July 18	Northfield, Minnesota – St. Peter's Lutheran Church 100th Anniversary
September 18	Minneapolis, Minnesota Solørlaget Stevne

1994 – Performances

June 19	Lanesboro, Minnesota Arts in the Park Festival
June 25	Fargo, North Dakota – Trollwood Park Seventeenth Annual Hjemkomst Festival
July 10	Chisholm, Minnesota – Iron Range Interpretative Center
August 7	Elbow Lake, Minnesota Flekkefjord Fest
August 20	Appleton, Minnesota Swift County Fair
August 31	St. Paul, Minnesota – State Fair Grounds (Borgs, Humphreys, Doerings, and Carlsons)
September 13	St. Paul, Minnesota Synnove-Nordkap Lodge Meeting

1995 – Performances

October 13-15	Lindsborg, Kansas – (five performances) Svensk Hyllningsfest

1996 – Performances

June 15	Choice, Minnesota – Hansen's Shed Alice & Orval Lea's Fiftieth Wedding Anniversary
July 26	Watertown, Minnesota – Downtown
	Minnesota History Center – Wedding Reception St. Paul, Minnesota

1997 – Performances

May 17	Atwater, Minnesota – Street Syttende Mai Celebration
	Cokato, Minnesota Church Anniversary
October	Lindsborg, Kansas Svensk Hyllningsfest

1998 – Performances

June 26-28	Estes Park, Colorado Scandinavian Midsummer Festival
July 12	Minneapolis, Minnesota Norway Day
	Benson, Minnesota Sons of Norway

1999 – Performances

May 13   Milan, Minnesota
                Syttende Mai Celebration

May 30   Dassel, Minnesota – Nordlie's Yard
                Memorial Day Hog Roast with Dancing

September 18   Willmar, Minnesota
                Celebrate Art! Celebrate Coffee! Festival

2000 – Performances

June 23-25   Estes Park, Colorado
                Scandinavian Midsummer Festival

August 5   Chippewa County – Swensson Farm Museum
                Norsk Reise Fest

October 8   Glenwood, Minnesota – Central Square
                Sons of Norway Viking Fair

2001 – Performances

May 13   Monticello, Minnesota
                Little Mountain Settlement

June 24   Terrace Mill, Minnesota
                Heritage Festival

June 28   Dassel, Minnesota – Covenant Church
                Midsommer Celebration

                Stewart, Minnesota

August 18   Paynesville, Minnesota

October 12-14 Lindsborg, Kansas
                Svensk Hyllningsfest

2002 – Performances

January 26   St. Peter, Minnesota
                Nursing Home Performance

May 18   Wanamingo, Minnesota
                Sons of Norway Syttende Mai Celebration

June 8   Buffalo, Minnesota
                Wright County Historical Society

June 15   Long Prairie, Minnesota

June 29-30   Estes Park, Colorado
                Scandinavian Festival

July 12	Northfield, Minnesota – St. Olaf College 7-Lag Stevne

2003 – Performances

April	Minneapolis, Minnesota – Radisson South Vesterheim's Museum Fundraiser
May 3	Minneapolis, Minnesota – Radisson South Federation of Women State Convention
June 28-29	Estes Park, Colorado Scandinavian Midsummer Festival
August 22	Dassel, Minnesota – Ergot Building Dassel Historical Society
	Little Falls, Minnesota
September 23	Alexander, Minnesota – Mount Carmel Senior Retreat

2004- Performances

June 19	Moose Lake, Minnesota Midsummer Celebration
June 20	Mora, Minnesota – Fairview School Auditorium Midsummer Festival
June 23	Dassel, Minnesota – Covenant Church Midsummer Festival
June	Highland Prairie, Fillmore County, Minnesota 150th Anniversary of the Church
July 27	Hutchinson, Minnesota – Oakes on Century Senior Care Center Program
December 11	Spicer, Minnesota – Greenlake Bible Camp Green Lake Lutheran Ministries Juletrefest

2005 – Performances

May 7	Monticello, Minnesota – Monticello High School Monticello Arts Council
May	Milan, Minnesota – Syttende Mai Celebration
June 12	Dassel, Minnesota – Ergot Building Dassel Historical Society Fundraiser
August	Elbow Lake, Minnesota Flekkefest (1st Sunday in August)
	Mankato, Minnesota Sons of Norway

November 12   Lakeville, Minnesota
               Sons of Norway Norsota Twentieth Anniversary

2006 – Performances
April 22   Sauk Center, Minnesota
               Scandinavian Smorgåsbord/Heritage Style Show

June 25   Dassel, Minnesota – Ergot Building
               Dassel Historical Society with Smorgasbord

September 17   Spicer, Minnesota – Green Lake Bible Camp
               Nordfjordlag Stevne

October 9   Willmar, Minnesota
               Sons of Norway

2007 – Performances
May 17   Willmar, Minnesota
               Syttende Mai Celebration and Parade

June 25   Starbuck, Minnesota
               Sons of Norway – Midsummer

2008 – Performances
May 10   Hutchinson, Minnesota

May 17   Milan, Minnesota
               Syttende Mai Celebration

May 18   Owatonna, Minnesota
               Sons of Norway Syttende Mai Celebration

October 12   St. Cloud, Minnesota
               Stearns Historical Museum

2009 – Performances
January 23   Cokato, Minnesota – Cokato Assisted Living

May 9   Lakeville, Minnesota – Sons of Norway Norsota

May 16   Milan, Minnesota
               Syttende Mai Celebration

July 17   Dassel, Minnesota
               Millner Winery

October 12   Willmar, Minnesota
               Sons of Norway

October 24   Willmar, Minnesota – Holiday Inn Convention
               SMAHC Annual Meeting

November 28   Dassel, Minnesota – Ergot Building
               Taste of Dassel

2010 – Performances
February   Dassel, Minnesota – PAC Center
               D-C Arts Association Celebration Showcase

March 16   Waconia, Minnesota
               Sons of Norway

May 15   Stoughton, Wisconsin
               Syttende Mai Celebration

June 18   Mora, Minnesota
               Midsummer Festival

August 26   Dassel, Minnesota – Mushroom Building
               Dassel Historical Society

September 19   Spicer, Minnesota – Green Lake Bible Camp
               Nordfjordlag 100th Anniversary

September 25   Waconia, Minnesota – Lake Waconia Regional
               Nordic Music Festival

September 26   Dassel, Minnesota – Gethsemane Lutheran
               Fundraiser

October 10   Willmar, Minnesota
               Sons of Norway

November 13   Dassel, Minnesota – Ergot Building
               Taste of Dassel

2011 – Performances
March 20   Hutchinson, Minnesota – Peace Lutheran
               Empty Nesters

May 14   Milan, Minnesota
               Syttende Mai Celebration

May 17   Benson, Minnesota
               Sons of Norway – Syttende Mai Celebration

October 2   Kimball, Minnesota – Millner Heritage Winery
               Oktoberfest and Grape Stomp

APPENDIX C

People Who Have Danced with the Dassel Leikarring

Charles and Karen Humphrey
Karna Humphrey
Barbara Kay
Heather Barbaro
Daniel and Carolyn Holje
Derek Holje
Craig Holje
David and Sharon Borg
Tim Borg
Ron Nelson (accordion player)
Joyce and Wilbert Carlson
John and Louise Tjernagel
Amy Tjernagel Wriedt
Leatrice and Ewald Nielsen
Bonita Garthus
Suzanne Asplin
David and Heidi Guennigsman
Earl and Ronette Doering
Dennis and Elaine Ashburn

David and Linda Fimrite
Jim and Lois Weeks
Cliff and Bonnie Eng
Clint and Brenda Lindquist
David and Linda Thompson
David and Mechelle Pitchford
Daniel Pitchford
Lorraine Pitchford Jensen
Sandy and Bob Dopkins
Howard and Marlene
    Amundson
Elaine and Kjell Nordlie
Catherine Nordlie Young
Tim and Helen Kringle
Joel and Marylou Swedberg
Gerald and Ann Bollman
Sara Bollman Nelson
Sheryl Swenson (Faust) and
    Bruce Swenson

The Dassel Leikarring Remembers the Little Mountain Settlement

The invitation to Little Mountain Settlement came in early May. And if we could, we were happy to be part of their Norwegian celebration. It was not an easy day for us, this certain Sunday in mid-May. There was church first. Many of us sang in the choir, one of us was the pastor; several of us had children to worry about. Then we raced home, had a quick bite to eat, and changed into our Leikarring costumes. We scrambled into the car and began the forty mile drive to Monticello, hoping the traffic would be agreeable for a group of people on a deadline. And there were, inevitably, the questions: Did we have the right shoes? Did the men remember their kneebands? Did the women remember the appropriate aprons? Is the music ready? What numbers are we going to dance? Did someone bring a camera? Finally we arrived.

We pulled into the driveway, left our cars in the parking lot, and began the climb up the little mountain nodding our respects to Robert Jameson, an authentic American war hero who sat at the gate recording each visitor. After a short walk to the top, past the hedge, there was Marian with a hearty handshake to welcome us. We stepped into a place of quiet, of respect for things past, a place that honored folk craft and art, a place where life of work and hospitality were valued. An audience awaited us, seated on wooden benches around the performance area.

There was the fragrance of coffee, and lilacs, and lilies-of-the-valley. The temperature was often cool. The leaves were fresh out on the trees that were a canopy for performers and spectators alike. And the sun shone brilliantly against a perfect blue sky. Our music, whether live accordion or taped, was soon in place, and the air was filled with the gentle rhythms of old dances: *schottische*, *pols*, *reinlender*. Our steps were muted on the lawn. Our red and black costumes were a bright contrast to the weathered historic buildings. As we watched each other across the circle to make sure our lines were straight, it seemed as if everything belonged, everything fit: buildings, dancers, audience, music, sunlight, trees. We were all indigenous to this place.

After dancing we had time to look around the settlement. We ducked our heads low as we entered each building. We ran our fingers over the rough grain in logs hewn more than a hundred years before. Each structure had something to say to us, something we could learn from, including similar tools and appliances and books used by our immigrant grandparents.

Later the Jamesons shared their feast of foods. It was a feast for a sacred family holiday, all the Jameson family came home to help celebrate their Norwegian heritage. They welcomed us as part of their family, too. In our memories it will always be spring at the Little Mountain Settlement. And it will remain in our memories a place where, on a Sunday in mid-May, life slowed down for an afternoon as we passed by the hedge into a place where we could walk and touch the buildings of people who brought the very customs we practice and cherish today. We will always remember how we were welcomed by the Jamesons, a family who treasured the things that mean the most.

Karen A. Humphrey, 2001

A Family Sampler

Genealogy is an interest of Many Leikarring members. Here's a sampler from some of the families.

Amund Haraldsen Garthus, the grandfather of Bonita Garthus and Suzanne Garthus Asplin, was from the Garthus Valley near Bagn in Valdres. He immigrated to America about 1880, settling in Independence, Trempeauleau County, Wisconsin.

John Tjernagel's family immigrated to the U.S. in 1898 from Sveo, Bua, in an area known as Tjernagel south of Haugasand. They settled in Ames, Story City, and Randall, Iowa. John and Louise visited the ancestral area in Norway and found it to be very hilly and rocky—not at all like Iowa or the New London, Minnesota area where John grew up. Several of John's Norwegian cousins work on oil rigs in the North Sea.

Leatrice Hoover Nielsen's great-grandparents, Håvard Eivindson Fylken Høyme and Berte Larsdotter Lomen Løkjisbergo, came from Vestre Slidre, Valdres, Oppland, in 1848. They traveled from New York to Dane County, Wisconsin, to the Norwegian colony of Koshkonong. In 1853, they moved to Locust in Plesaant Township, Winnesiek County, Iowa, where they lived the rest of their lives. On the other side of her family, Ole Olson Fåberg and Synneva Bergitte Olsdotter Bjelland met in Bergen, Norway, where they lived for a year before coming to the U.S. in 1871 to New Hampton, Chickasaw County, Iowa, where other relatives had settled. Most of them took the last name of Thompson.

Bonnie Berg Eng discovered that her roots go back to Tingvoll, Norway, in Mor og Romsdal. Her father's father's family immigrated in 1892 to Superior, Wisconsin, but moved to Minneapolis in the 1930s. Her father's mother's people came to Superior from the area around Oslo in the 1880s. Her mother's mother was from Arvika, Sweden, but her mother's father, perhaps, was a victim of the border shift and family legend says that he was born in Norway, but raised in Sweden. Cliff's ancestors came from Edleskog, Dalsland, Sweden, in 1893 and settled in Buffalo, Minnesota. Cliff's mother's mother came from Angermanland in the far northeast region of Sweden.

Dennis and Elaine Anderson Asburn are both of Swedish heritage. Dennis' people came from Småland—his grandmother, Augusta Mina Peterson, was born in the Tranemo parish; his great-grandmother, Christina Lind Neal, was born there in 1837. Elaine's great-great-grandfather was Olaf Magnuson, born in 1844 in Vastra Torsas, Kronoberg. Another great-grandfather, Anders John (Jonasson), who changed his name to Andrew Anderson, was born in 1853 in Ostergotland, and emigrated in 1866. Her great-grandmother, Elizabeth Berg, born in 1857 in Bredsattra on the island of Oland, came to the United States in 1866 when she was nine years old. Elaine's father's people came from Västergotland and Skephult parish in Alfsborg. "I still have my grandfather's steerage contract for $28.50 and a copy of his citizenship papers from May 1906."

Elaine Lea Nordlie has long been a family genealogist. Her people were in the early wave of immigrants from Norway to Wisconsin, then to Fillmore County, Minnesota. Here's her family history:

Aaste Amundsdatter Hjamdal (1830-1902) emigrated from Lunde in Telemark with her parents, Anund Erickson and Liv Olavsdatter, and siblings in 1844. They settled first in the Skoponong settlement in Wisconsin, and in 1854 moved to Fillmore County, Minnesota. Aaste's husband, Hans Gunnarson Lia (1820-1900), emigrated from Kviteseid, Telemark in 1852, settled in the Skoponong settlement, then moved to Fillmore County in 1854.

Aaste's sister, Taran Amundsdatter Hjamdal (1832-1892), married Mikkel Kittelson Jordgrav (1829-1910) who emigrated from Kviteseid with his parents, Kittel Olavson Jordgrav and Margit Mikkelsdatter Øygarden, and siblings in May 1843. They also settled at Skoponong, moved to Highland Prairie, Fillmore County, in 1854. After Mikkel served in the Civil War, they moved to Cottonwood County, Minnesota.

Anna Jacobsdatter (1851-1900), emigrated from Lom with her husband, Nils Johnson Marstein (1849-1916), and their son. They settled in Fillmore County.

Mikkel Olson Rekanes (1838-1890) emigrated from Flaabygd, Telemark with his parents, Ole Mikkelson Rekanes and Birgith Kittelsdatter Dompendal (1813-?), and siblings in 1853. They lived in rural Whalan, Fillmore County. Mikkel married Margit Olavsdatter Lone (1834-1890), who emigrated from Tuddal, Telemark.

Gunnhild Kirstine Neilsdatter (1832-1894) emigrated from the Hasselied farm in Bamble, Telemark, with her husband, Thor Kittelsen Hasselied (1838-1911), and two sons. They settled in rural Whalan.

Botolf Pederson Ramsøy (1833-?) emigrated from Gudvangen, Norway, in 1867 with his wife, Gertrude Mikkelsdatter (1832-?), and children. They settled first in Winnebago County, Iowa, then in Fillmore County.

Elaine's grandfather, Rasmus Berekvam (1898-1957), emigrated from Stavanger in 1914 and settled in Whalen. Rasmus married Cora Hasliet, the granddaughter of Botolf Pederson Ramsøy, Gertrude Mikkelsdatter, Gunhild Kirstine Nielsdatter, and Thor Kittelsen Hasselied.

In one of the bedrooms in their Dassel home, Elaine created a heritage room with family mementos and portraits. Many who are beneficiaries of the Nordlies hospitality enjoy hearing the family stories.